# THE POTOMAC RIVER

# THE
# POTOMAC
# RIVER

## A HISTORY & GUIDE

GARRETT PECK

Charleston · London

THE
History
PRESS

Published by The History Press
Charleston, SC  29403
www.historypress.net

*Cover images*: Front: Jefferson Rock. *Library of Congress*; Great Falls. *Garrett Peck*. Back: Piney Point Lighthouse. *Garrett Peck*; colorful kayaks. *Garrett Peck*; view of Washington Monument from the Netherlands Carillon. *Garrett Peck*.

First published 2012

Manufactured in the United States

ISBN 978.1.60949.600.5

Library of Congress Cataloging-in-Publication Data

Peck, Garrett.
The Potomac River : a history and guide / Garrett Peck
p. cm.
Includes bibliographical references and index.
ISBN 978-1-60949-600-5
1.  Potomac River--History. 2.  Potomac River Region--History. 3.  Potomac River Region-
-History, Local. 4.  Historic sites--Potomac River Region. 5.  Potomac River Region--
Guidebooks.  I. Title.
F187.P8P32 2012
975.2--dc23
2012002973

*Notice*: The information in this book is true and complete to the best of our knowledge. It is offered without guarantee on the part of the author or The History Press. The author and The History Press disclaim all liability in connection with the use of this book.

# Contents

# Acknowledgements

A book isn't an individual contribution but rather a collaboration among many people and their expertise. I'm in debt to so many for their time and assistance. Two of the leading conservation organizations dedicated to the Potomac and Anacostia Rivers provided invaluable support: Anne Sundermann and Deanna Tricarico of the Potomac Conservancy and Brent Bolin and Emily Gillespie of the Anacostia Watershed Society.

Kim Lloyd of Seneca Creek State Park gave me key guidance on how to visit the Seneca quarry, an unmarked site that is historically rich and nationally significant. May there one day be interpretive signs and trails for that quarry! Thanks as well to George Tabb, the park manager at the Ball's Bluff Battlefield, and to Rebecca Roberts and Tim Krepp of Congressional Cemetery, one of the great gems of Washington. Judy Feldman of the National Coalition to Save Our Mall allowed me to bounce ideas about the National Mall, and I'm so appreciative for her insight.

Two of the more interesting and unusual tours involved how Washington, D.C., treats its water. Tom Jacobus and Patty Gamby filled me in on the details of Washington Aqueduct—the U.S. Army Corps of Engineers agency that provides D.C.'s tap water. Mark Ramirez led a fun and fascinating tour of Blue Plains (who knew sewage treatment could be so interesting!). Thanks as well to Alex Hirschhorn of D.C. Water.

Numerous friends who helped with my previous book, *Prohibition in Washington, D.C.*, stepped up once again (it was like getting the band back together!). I turned to Kenny Allen for his creative mapmaking skills, and once again he impressed with his beautiful maps. Cindy Janke provided her intimate knowledge of the history of Capitol Hill and the Anacostia region. John DeFerrari generously provided the historic postcards on the cover. Thanks to my commissioning editor at The History Press, Hannah Cassilly, for taking another chance with me, and to Ryan Finn for his great copyediting skills. Lastly, thanks to my parents for a fun author photo. No authors were harmed in the making of this book.

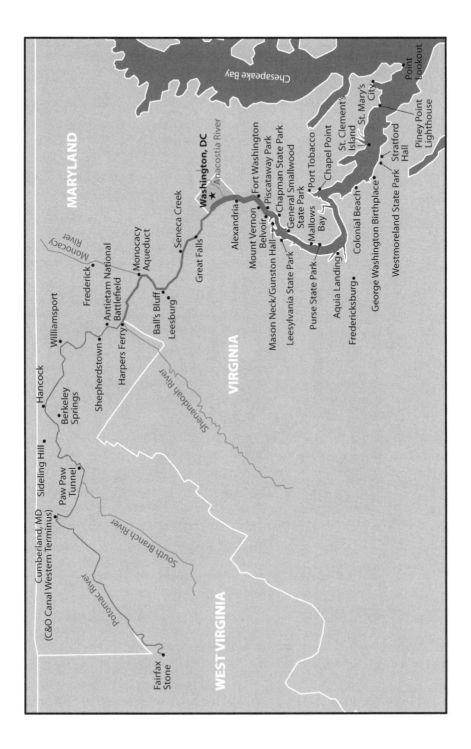

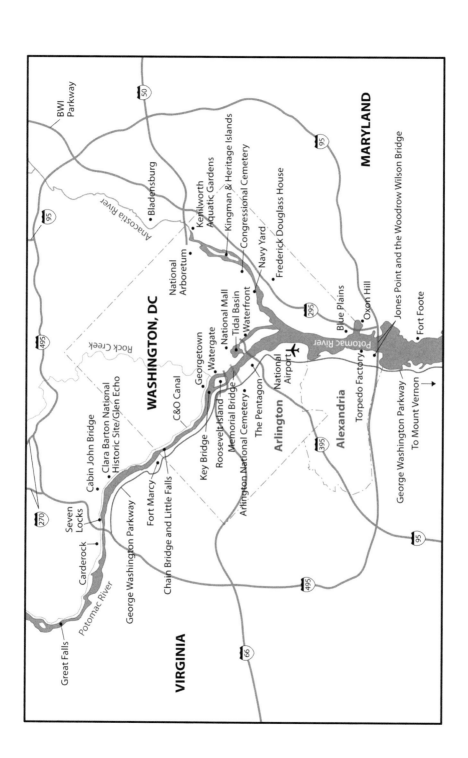

# ORIGINS

Father Andrew White, a Jesuit priest who traveled with the first English Catholic settlers to Maryland in 1634, wrote about seeing the Potomac: "Never have I seen a larger or more beautiful river." European settlers were amazed at the river's bountiful fish, forested banks and rich soil. Indian villages dotted its banks. This land would nurture and sustain colonists and the early American republic and eventually provide the seat for the national government, Washington, D.C.

The story of the Potomac is the story of our country: colonization, commerce, economic development, war, pollution, restoration, conservation and resource management, historic preservation and recreation. The Potomac is the nation's river.

The river is remarkably intact, spared from channelization that permanently scarred so many of our nation's rivers. Much of its shores are publicly owned or held in conservation trust. Where else on earth can one see bald eagles or a raging river gorge just miles from a major urban center? This river also provides 80 percent of the water to more than 5 million inhabitants of the Washington metropolitan area.

This is both a history and a guidebook for exploring the Potomac River. It provides an overview of the best places to explore from historic and natural perspectives that are likewise accessible to the general public. There are many sites to explore within an hour's drive from Washington, D.C.—some, such as Great Falls and Mason Neck, are within half an hour from downtown. This book is organized along geographic lines, starting at the river's origin at the Fairfax Stone and ending at Point Lookout.

# A Natural History of the Potomac

The Potomac starts six miles north of Thomas, West Virginia, on the Allegheny Plateau, 3,140 feet above sea level. This lies at the foot of Backbone Mountain, Maryland's highest point. The Potomac is 383 miles long. The first 275 miles course through the Allegheny and Blue Ridge Mountains, a wild river that finally calms into a tidal estuary at Georgetown. The river then flows 108 miles to its 11-mile-wide mouth, where it meets the lower Chesapeake Bay.

But this is the Potomac we see today. There have been many ancestor rivers over the millennia. The region that the Potomac flows through—and in fact exposes—is some of the oldest land in the world. The Potomac tells the geological history of the world.

So how was the river formed? The Mid-Atlantic region was once largely under water or at sea level. Some of the oldest rocks along the Potomac are the cliffs at Carderock, which initially formed about 450 million years ago as underwater volcanic sediment under the ocean Iapetus—the forerunner to the Atlantic. The ocean gradually closed as Africa pressed up against North America about 250 million years ago to form the supercontinent Pangaea, compressing the sediment into mica rocks. The same pressure also created the Appalachian and Allegheny Mountains. These were once sedimentary coastal plains, but they were pushed up into tall mountains. As the continents divided, the Atlantic Ocean formed, but the rocks once underwater were now above ground and part of North America.

Rain fell on the new mountains, and streams like the Potomac eroded the Appalachians into the series of ridges we see today. The Sideling Hill road cut near Hancock, Maryland, features a cutaway of the earth's crust, exposing hundreds of millions of years of geologic history. Harpers Ferry is another ancient site that shows the power of erosion.

There are six major physiographic regions along the course of the Potomac River:

## Allegheny Plateau Province

The Potomac begins in West Virginia at 3,140 feet above sea level. This province is very rugged, characterized by steep hillsides and narrow valleys. The river drops 2,000 feet in its first forty-six miles. The Allegheny Plateau is coal-rich, and there are many mines. For this reason, the North Branch is polluted from the highly acidic coal mine runoff. The seven-mile-long Jennings Randolph Reservoir was constructed to control acidity and conserve drinking water. The river plunges down the plateau near Keyser, West Virginia.

## RIDGE AND VALLEY PROVINCE

This is a series of steep parallel ridges and hairpin curves on the Potomac. Rivers and streams that form in the region, such as the South Branch and Cacapon River, cut through beds of shale and limestone, both easily erodible. The Sideling Hill Road Cut on Interstate 68 shows the many sedimentary layers of the province.

## GREAT VALLEY PROVINCE

The Potomac bisects this province between Hancock, Maryland, and Harpers Ferry. A fertile valley with thin soil and protruding limestone supports small farms, as you'll see around Antietam National Battlefield. The Shenandoah River flows through the province.

## BLUE RIDGE PROVINCE

The Shenandoah River joins the Potomac at Harpers Ferry at the base of the Blue Ridge Mountains. The combined rivers then flow through a water gap carved in the mountains. It is a breathtaking scene, best viewed from Jefferson Rock, the Point at Harpers Ferry or atop Loudoun Heights.

## PIEDMONT PROVINCE

This is a landscape of rolling hillsides. The Monocacy River is the largest tributary within this province. A transitional fall zone begins at Great Falls, as the river has carved the fifteen-mile Potomac Gorge, lined with palisade-like cliffs such as Mather Gorge and Carderock. The river drops 140 feet in elevation. The Piedmont's eastern boundary is the end of the fall line, which includes Little Falls and the backbone ridge through Arlington County, Virginia.

## COASTAL PLAIN PROVINCE

Also known as the Tidewater region, this begins at Georgetown and is nearly at sea level. The Potomac widens to a calm, navigable river along its last third until it reaches the Chesapeake Bay, 101 miles away at Point Lookout. The river here is an estuary, meaning that it is tidal. The water becomes more brackish as it approaches the Chesapeake.

It took several ice ages to shape the Potomac Valley. The glaciers never reached the Mid-Atlantic, but they devoured so much water that ocean levels fell and rivers shrank into trickles. The ice reached its maximum extent about twenty thousand years ago. At Great Falls, the river once coursed through a calmer streambed where the Widewater is now. As the last ice age came to an end, melting ice turned trickling streams into raging rivers. The Potomac broke through the terrace at Great Falls and carved a new channel for itself about ten thousand years ago—the deep trench that we call Mather Gorge—just below the waterfall.

The Potomac and its major tributaries (South Branch, Shenandoah, Monocacy, Anacostia and Occoquan Rivers), along with its minor tributaries (Savage, Cacapon, Wicomico and St. Mary's Rivers; Conococheague, Opequon, Antietam, Goose, Seneca and Rock Creeks) and dozens of smaller streams, drain some 14,670 square miles of land in the District of Columbia, Maryland, Pennsylvania, Virginia and West Virginia. More than half of the watershed is forested, and only 10 percent is developed.

The Potomac is rich in life, fostered by fields of underwater grasses that provide hiding places for small fish and oxygen for all things that live. Alewife herring, eel, perch, rockfish, shad and smallmouth bass are native to the river. Many of these are migratory fish, traveling upriver to spawn in tributaries like Rock Creek. The river is also full of invasive species, including largemouth bass, carp, blue catfish and snakeheads, an ugly southeast Asian fish that began encroaching in the river in 2004.

The Potomac is a favorite stopover for migrating birds. Hundreds of bird species live along the river. Among the most recognizable are bald eagles, blue heron, Canada geese, cormorants, ducks, kingfishers and osprey. These feast on the plentiful fish and grasses. Other domesticated birds are causing environmental concerns for the Potomac, notably farm-raised chickens. Agricultural runoff from poultry farms and sediment from urban development pollute the river. The Potomac is far from pristine.

## A HUMAN HISTORY OF THE POTOMAC

The name Potomac comes from an Algonquin Indian word and has many spellings and translations, including "where goods are brought in," "they are coming by water" and, perhaps most appropriately, "great trading place."

Along the Tidewater, the Piscataways dominated the Maryland side of the river, while the Powhatan Confederacy controlled the Virginia side. The Allegheny Mountains were Shawnee territory, though boundaries between tribes were often fluid. The Indians used the rivers as highways, and their fishing, hunting and village sites were seasonal. They also grew crops such as corn and tobacco and made stone tools along Aquia Creek.

Few of the Indian tribes on the Tidewater remained on their lands long after first contact with European settlers, and it is only more recently that we've rediscovered how well populated and strong Indian culture was along the Potomac. In the 1930s and 1940s, a Piscataway village was excavated, and it became one of the most significant Indian finds along the Potomac. The size of the Accokeek Creek Site indicated that the Piscataways were powerful, though they had many enemies, notably the Iroquois and the Susquehannocks. By the end of the seventeenth century, the Piscataways had lost most of their power and lands to European settlers.

In 1607, Jamestown was established as the first English settlement in Virginia. A year later, Captain John Smith led a party of fourteen men up the Potomac to look for a northwest passage through the continent. He found the river teeming with fish, as well as many tribes of Indians fishing and trading along the river. He ventured up the river as far as Great Falls. Back in England four years later, Smith published *A General History of Virginia* that included a regional map with its many Indian villages.

The Potomac resides almost entirely in Maryland, according to the land grant King Charles I of England gave to Cecil Calvert, Lord Baltimore, in 1632. The border is the mean low-water mark on the *south* bank of the Potomac. His son, King Charles II, gave another major land grant, the Northern Neck Propriety, to the Fairfax family on the Virginia side of the river.

The first 140 English Catholic settlers bound for Maryland arrived in 1634 in two ships, the *Ark* and the *Dove*. They landed on St. Clement's Island and settled at St. Mary's. This set the stage for conflict with the Anglicans and Puritans of the colonies, who widely detested Catholicism. Maryland became the first colony to codify religious toleration, but that was short-lived—the royal governor soon drove the Catholics underground. It wasn't until the Maryland state constitution, written during the American Revolution, that tolerance was enshrined.

As the first arrivals had settled prime Tidewater properties for growing tobacco, subsequent immigrants looked west for fertile lands. In 1748, the

Captain John Smith explored the Potomac region in 1608 and then published a history and map of Virginia four years later in England. *Library of Congress.*

Ohio Company was created to settle the Ohio River Valley. King George II granted it 500,000 acres west of the Alleghenies. The Potomac was the obvious avenue to these lands. The company established an outpost at Wills Creek (now Cumberland, Maryland) to begin a trail into the Ohio Country. However, the French got there first, moving in from Canada to build forts along Lake Erie and, most importantly, at Fort Duquesne (now Pittsburgh) at the juncture of three rivers. The conflict was set for the French and Indian War (1755–63), which resulted in the French eviction from North America. Part of the peace settlement promised the Indians that the colonists would not settle beyond the mountains, something that infuriated the Americans, who had big plans for the West.

George Washington and Robert E. Lee were both born along the banks of the Potomac's coastal plain. Washington's home, Mount Vernon, is the most recognizable building on the river, and it is Washington who looms far larger than anyone over the Potomac's history. He saw the

Potomac as a gateway to open the West to commerce and development. He helped organize the Potowmack Company in 1785 to improve the river for trade; brokered an interstate commerce agreement known as the Mount Vernon Compact; selected the national capital site, which was later named after him; and chose Harpers Ferry for the nation's new armory.

Washington's motives weren't entirely altruistic: he picked the site of the new federal city because it was close to his Mount Vernon estate. He sponsored the Potowmack Company not just because it was good for the country but because he had significant landholdings in the Ohio Country and wanted them to appreciate.

The Potomac was a key theater of fighting during the War of 1812 between Great Britain and the United States. After American forces burned the Canadian capital of York (now Toronto) in 1813, the British decided to exact revenge on Washington, D.C. The Royal Navy sailed up the Chesapeake Bay and Patuxent River, depositing a small army at Benedict that then marched overland to attack the city. On August 25, 1814, the British defeated the American army in a short battle at Bladensburg and then burned the public buildings like the Capitol, the President's House (later the White House), arsenal, treasury and war departments, as well as the Long Bridge over the Potomac. The Americans burned the Washington Navy Yard to keep the British from seizing its ships and supplies. This was only a raid: the British soon returned to their fleet. Meanwhile, another Royal Navy squadron sailed up the Potomac. It accepted Alexandria's surrender, seized a large amount of supplies and then sailed downriver. The British were soon repulsed at Baltimore.

Tobacco was the cash crop along the Potomac's coastal plain. Maryland and Virginia imported African slaves to work the farms, fields and plantations. Tobacco quickly depleted the soil, and slash-and-burn farming led to deforestation that rapidly silted up streams. "Tobacco cultivation was the strip-mining of its day," wrote historian Fergus Bordewich. The Potomac likewise proved an avenue of escape for many African slaves. The Underground Railroad developed as a clandestine network for slaves to escape north to Canada, helped along the way by "conductors." Washington was often a stop along the route, a southern city with many abolitionists and free blacks.

The Potowmack Company failed to provide a reliable trade route, as the Potomac was unpredictable with its droughts and floods. Investors ventured on a year-round solution: the Chesapeake & Ohio Canal, which was intended to link Washington to Pittsburgh. Begun in 1828, it reached the halfway point, Cumberland, Maryland, in 1850, and there construction ended. The canal operated for ninety-six years until the great flood of 1924 closed it.

At 184.5 miles long, the C&O Canal parallels nearly half of the Potomac's distance like a needle and a very long string. Mike High, author of *The C&O Canal Companion*, called it "a forested path through two and a half centuries of history." It is an architectural and engineering wonder with its seventy-four locks, eleven aqueducts and 160 culverts. Canalboats were standardized at ninety feet in length to fit into the locks, and each could carry 125 tons. They were pulled by teams of mules.

Canal traffic on the C&O peaked in 1871. The canal's decline matched that of small industry along the Potomac until virtually all of it shut down. Besides railroads, the C&O's chief adversaries were periodic floods on the Potomac that devastated the canal. A huge flood in 1889 closed the canal for eighteen months and sent it into bankruptcy. The B&O Railroad took over its operations.

A catalytic event that helped trigger the Civil War occurred on the Potomac: in October 1859, abolitionist John Brown seized the U.S. Arsenal at Harpers Ferry in an attempt to start a slave insurrection. The raid failed, but it so irrevocably split North and South that the war began less than eighteen months later.

Many Civil War battles and skirmishes were fought along the river: Ball's Bluff and Antietam, as well as a Confederate blockade of the Potomac. The river had an army named after it: the Army of the Potomac, the largest Union army that fought to defeat the Confederacy and its leading general, Robert E. Lee. It fought Lee to a draw at Antietam, achieved a decisive victory at Gettysburg, besieged him at Richmond and Petersburg and finally forced his surrender at Appomattox in 1865.

The Potomac divided the Confederacy from the Union. However, it is not the famed Mason-Dixon line—that is actually the border between Maryland and Pennsylvania, set in 1764. Both Delaware and Maryland were slave states that remained part of the Union. The highlands of western Maryland had few slaves and were pro-Union, while the Tidewater was tobacco country and ripe with secessionists. Had Maryland seceded, it would have left Washington inside the Confederacy, an untenable situation, and thus President Abraham Lincoln suspended the writ of habeas corpus to arrest Southern sympathizers and prevent the state from seceding.

## THE POTOMAC'S CLOSE CALL

The Potomac was crowded with shipping when Alexandria, Georgetown and Washington were active ports, but commercial traffic on the river faded after World War II. The many danger points on the river were marked with lighthouses; every one of the hexagonal structures has been lost over the years. Today, there are only five surviving lighthouses on the Potomac: Point Lookout, Piney Point, Blackistone, Fort Washington and Jones Point. All are in the Tidewater region.

In the twentieth century, the U.S. Army Corps of Engineers straightened and deepened the channels of many American rivers to make them navigable. These costly alterations forever changed the ecosystems of many rivers, such as the Mississippi. These once flowed freely, constantly changing their course, building sandbars, eroding banks and depositing silt in their estuaries to built new land and support aquatic life. The corps' role was to subdue rivers to support shipping.

In the 1950s, the corps proposed a series of fourteen dams to tame the Potomac and provide drinking water for the Washington region's growing population. This would create numerous lakes while flooding many of the historic sites and recreation areas, such as Harpers Ferry. Public outcry shelved the plan, and only two dams were built: the Little Falls Dam in 1959, which only creates a small pool of water, and the Bloomington Dam, started in 1971.

What is unusual about the Potomac is that much of the river is natural. The Potomac is largely a free-flowing river with few levees on it and only a handful of dams, including the Washington Aqueduct Dam and a few remaining C&O Canal dams. There certainly was once industry along its banks, particularly sparked by the C&O Canal and Washington Navy Yard, but that largely died off.

Rivers will wander. It is their nature. It is a myth to believe that we can tame the waters of our world. Rather than trying to contain a river through levees—which will eventually fail—it is best to understand that rivers naturally flood from time to time and build our cities and farms accordingly.

Washington never became a great river port like Baltimore, New York or Philadelphia. And the Potomac turned out to be not such a great route to the west—the river is too wild and unpredictable. Historian Joel Achenbach, writing in *The Grand Idea*, noted how fortunate we are that the Potomac is natural and largely intact:

*The failure of Washington's plan was the best thing that ever happened to the river. The Potomac has survived, so far, the attempts to make it useful in the traditional sense. It has overcome the schemes of Founding Fathers, canal-builders, railroad magnates, coal-mining conglomerates, power companies, sewage treatment authorities, highway planners, and the Army Corps of Engineers. The best use of the river, it turns out, is to let it be a river.*

## Saving the C&O Canal

A massive Potomac flood in 1924 closed the C&O Canal permanently, and the canal was largely abandoned for thirty years. Maintenance ended and the canal deteriorated. Another tremendous flood, called the Record Flood, hit the Potomac in 1936. Washington escaped flooding only by building a line of sandbags on the Mall. Congress purchased the C&O in 1938 from the B&O Railroad for $2 million (a fraction of the $11 million it had cost to build) and transferred it to the National Park Service.

Two proposals emerged to put the canal to use: build a tourist railroad from Great Falls to Cumberland or pave the canal. The latter would create a two-lane highway above Great Falls, similar to the George Washington Memorial Parkway. The canal would be restored from Georgetown to Great Falls, leaving just that small section intact. The environmental and historical preservation movement was just beginning. Until then, it was natural to simply tear down old structures for something new. The Department of the Interior, which runs the National Park Service, opted to pave the canal in 1950. Most of the C&O would be no more.

There was a backlash to the plan, and fortunately, one high-profile Washingtonian drew attention to the canal's plight: Supreme Court justice William O. Douglas. He was an outdoorsman and a hiker who appreciated the canal for its recreational value. Two weeks after the *Washington Post* published an editorial supporting the paving effort, Douglas challenged the editors to go on a hike with him:

*I wish the man who wrote your editorial of January 3, 1954, approving the Parkway, would take time off and come with me. We would go with packs on our backs and walk the 185 miles to*

*Cumberland. I feel that if your editor did, he would return a new man and use the power of your great editorial page to help keep this sanctuary untouched.*

On March 8, Douglas, the editors and two dozen followers began the hike in Cumberland (they decided to walk downhill). They drew national attention. When they reached Georgetown eight days later, fifty thousand people cheered their arrival. It was a publicity stunt, but it worked. The newspapers changed their minds, and so did the public. The C&O Canal was saved; it would be preserved as a natural greenway and recreation area, with the towpath converted into a footpath for cyclists, hikers and runners. It was declared a national monument in 1961, and ten years later, President Richard Nixon signed the act creating the Chesapeake and Ohio Canal National Historical Park.

Today, the National Park Service operates six museums dedicated to the canal: Georgetown, Great Falls, Brunswick, Williamsport, Hancock and Cumberland. We are fortunate that the canal is protected as a national park, and thus much of the Potomac shoreline is in the public trust. The towpath is one of the best hiking and biking trails in the region. A popular day trip is to bike from Georgetown to Great Falls and back, about thirteen miles each way.

## From National Disgrace to Cleanup

By the 1960s, the Potomac was nearly a dead river, largely because of untreated sewage and highly acidic coal mine runoff. People were cautioned against swimming in it. In 1965, President Lyndon B. Johnson addressed Congress, calling the Potomac "a river of decaying sewage and rotten algae." He directed the Department of the Interior to create a conservation plan. The U.S. Army Corps of Engineers' plan to dam much of the river was effectively shelved.

Johnson's successor in the White House, Richard Nixon, signed the Clean Water Act of 1972, and the river began to heal. The federal government invested in upgraded sewage treatment facilities, notably Blue Plains but also others, and these sharply cut the amount of nitrogen and other chemicals in the water. The result is that the algae blooms shrank significantly, the water grasses returned and the fish population rebounded. In addition, the Bloomington Dam, built high on the

Allegheny Plateau and completed in 1981, helped control the acidic coal mine runoff. The Potomac began to heal.

Today, much of the threat to the river comes from development. Urban and suburban development creates a great deal of runoff of silt. Before parking lots and roads were built everywhere, rainwater naturally soaked into the earth, and an abundance of trees held soil in place. With urban drainage systems, rainwater from gutters, storm drains and impermeable surfaces like parking lots funnels into streams at high speed and volume, taking everything in its path (aquatic life, motor oil, plastic bags, soil, tennis balls and so on). This is called nonpoint pollution, since it has no single source. During the summer, heated pavement can warm water beyond the point that organisms can survive in streams.

In addition, combined sewer overflows (CSO) from older sewer systems deposit billions of gallons of raw sewage into the nation's rivers. This especially affects the Anacostia, which is dense with sewage and silt, a double whammy to what was once a pristine forty-foot-deep river.

A number of organizations and volunteer groups have emerged to oversee stewardship of the Potomac, its parks and its tributaries. The Interstate Commission on the Potomac River Basin was formed in 1940 as a regional partnership of states within the Potomac watershed to ensure an adequate drinking water supply and monitor the river's health. The Anacostia Watershed Society was organized in 1989 to champion cleanup of the Anacostia River, one of the most polluted rivers in the country.

The Potomac Conservancy is an accredited land trust, formed in 1993 to protect the river and our drinking water and conserve the land along it. It runs the River Center at Lock 8 to educate people about the river's ecology. It also sponsors annual river cleanups, native seed collections and trail restoration with thousands of volunteers. The Potomac Conservancy issues a letter grade for the river's health. In 2011, it downgraded the river's health from a D+ to a D, citing downstream development and upstream farming and forest loss.

Industrial-grade poultry farms in the Potomac watershed use antibiotics and hormones and create an enormous amount of manure and chemical-laden agricultural runoff. People are increasingly using antibacterial soap and medications, the residue of which flushes into our waterways. Researchers are noticing the rise of intersex fish in the Potomac, brought on by man-made pollutants. It will take more awareness, dedication and money to improve the Potomac's health.

The Potomac is a national treasure. Nurturing its health means protecting this dynamic river for future generations, as well as the rich bevy of historic sites along its banks. So let us start our journey down the Potomac at the river's beginning.

# FAIRFAX STONE HISTORICAL MONUMENT

In 1649, the exiled King Charles II of England granted seven supporters 5.28 million acres of land in Virginia. This land was the Northern Neck Proprietary, bordered by the Potomac River to the north and the Rappahannock River to the south. The western boundary was the Potomac's "first fountain."

In 1719, Lord Thomas Fairfax inherited all seven shares of the property, which became known as the Fairfax Land Grant. His interest was to find the northernmost branch of the Potomac so that he could have more land—as it was, the Northern Neck represented a quarter of Virginia's size. The colony dispatched a surveying team in 1736 to mark the boundary. Fairfax objected to its findings and sued.

The privy court in London sided with Fairfax in 1745. With the legal rights to the property in hand, he dispatched another surveying team the next year to map the Northern Neck. The team included Peter Jefferson, Thomas Jefferson's father. They installed the first Fairfax Stone, a rock with the initials "Fx" inscribed on it, at the source of the North Branch River. This expedition also marked the location of the "Medicinal Springs" where the colonial elite were congregating. This later became the town of Berkeley Springs.

Maryland took issue. According to the 1632 charter granted to Lord Baltimore, the Maryland border was the westernmost source of the Potomac. Governor Horatio Sharpe sent Thomas Cresap in 1752 to find the westernmost source of the Potomac. Cresap reported that the South Branch was, in fact, farther to the west.

Why didn't Maryland assert its proper claim? The French and Indian War broke out in 1755, and the disputed land was far away in Indian territory. Had Maryland asserted its rights, it would have recovered substantial territory in the mountains—at Virginia and Lord Fairfax's expense. Maryland finally sued West Virginia more than a century later, as that state was now on the disputed border. In 1910, the U.S. Supreme Court sided with West Virginia, and the traditional border has remained fixed on the North Branch.

There have been six Fairfax Stones, one replacing the next because of weather or graffiti. The current stone was installed in 1956. It is a six-ton rock with a flat face, on which is inlaid a historical inscription of the stone's importance. Next to it is the 1910 stone. A tiny trickle springs from the hillside, the origin of the Potomac River.

*How to get there: Fairfax Stone Historical Monument, part of a four-acre West Virginia state park, is six miles north of Thomas, West Virginia.*

# Canals and Commerce

The Potomac highlands of western Maryland are sparsely populated but rich in history and natural beauty. The river spills from the Allegheny Plateau and snakes through the Ridge and Valley Province. George Washington visited the region many times and saw it as a commercial highway to the West. But before Washington came legendary pioneer Thomas Cresap. The C&O Canal, the National Road and railroads helped open the region to development in the nineteenth century, and all converged at Cumberland, Maryland.

## Cumberland

Cumberland was founded in 1749 as the Wills Creek outpost for the Ohio Company. As the French beat the British to the Ohio Country, Maryland governor Horatio Sharpe ordered a large fort built to protect the outpost; it was named Fort Cumberland. The fort became the jumping-off point for British general Edward Braddock's disastrous expedition against Fort Duquesne in 1755 during the French and Indian War. Young George Washington, a newly minted colonel and Braddock's aide-de-camp, built his headquarters there in advance of Braddock's arrival. On July 9, Braddock's army was ambushed in the woods near the French fort (now Pittsburgh) and nearly wiped out. Braddock was killed. Washington rallied the survivors and led them out of the wilderness.

Cumberland is built along a curve in the Potomac. North of the city is a distinct cut in the surrounding mountains known as the Narrows, where Wills Creek flows between Wills and Haystack Mountains. Cumberland was a major transportation hub. It marks the beginning of the National Road (now U.S. 40), the country's first federally financed highway, begun in 1811. The B&O Railroad reached the town in 1842, beating the C&O Canal by eight years.

The C&O reached Cumberland in 1850 after its 184.5-mile journey from Georgetown. It was supposed to continue to Pittsburgh, but sapped of funds, construction ended. The canal's Cumberland Terminus, a major inland harbor with two basins, was built at the juncture of the Potomac and Wills Creek. Most of the canalboats were constructed there, and many of the canawlers called Cumberland their home.

What brought these highways to this town? Coal. A rich vein was discovered on George's Creek west of the city, and this became a significant source of commerce for the region—but also pollution that lingers with us today. In fact, the majority of freight hauled on the C&O was coal destined for Washington.

Wills Creek runs through Cumberland, Maryland. To the left is the Western Maryland Train and the 1907 railway station that houses the C&O Canal Western Terminus. *Garrett Peck.*

Cumberland was nicknamed the Queen City, as it was the second largest in Maryland after Baltimore. It is a city of church spires—they seem to be everywhere—and mid-nineteenth-century Victorian architecture. It is a beautiful city to walk through. The Washington Street Historic District includes several dozen stops on its walking tour, including Emmanuel Episcopal Church and its Tiffany stained-glass windows (16 Washington Street). The church was also a stop on the Underground Railroad that helped slaves escape to the north. It had a tunnel that linked to the C&O Canal, which was how many contraband slaves reached Cumberland. Emmanuel resides on the site of Fort Cumberland. The Fort Cumberland Trail is an interpretive path through the historic district that also includes Washington's headquarters.

The C&O Canal's Cumberland Visitor Center is located in the Western Maryland Railroad Station, built in 1913. The railroad offers three-hour excursions from Cumberland to Frostburg, Maryland.

Cumberland is the jumping-off point for the Great Allegheny Passage, a rails-to-trail system that continues 150 miles to Pittsburgh. One can bike from Pittsburgh to Washington, D.C., via the Great Allegheny Passage and C&O Canal towpath.

## The Battle of Folck's Mill

During the Civil War, Cumberland was a key transit point along the B&O Railroad, a strategic artery that linked the Union to the West. A large garrison was maintained there to protect the railroad.

After Confederate general Jubal Early's raid on Washington, D.C., in July 1864, he returned to secure the Shenandoah Valley. Early then launched a series of raids on the B&O Railroad and sent two cavalry brigades under John McCausland and Bradley Johnson to raid Chambersburg, Pennsylvania. When the citizens refused to pay a $100,000 ransom, the Confederates burned the town. They demanded a smaller ransom from Hancock, Maryland, but Union cavalry chased them off.

On August 1, the Confederates approached Cumberland from the east to wreck the B&O, only to be surprised by a Union force guarding Evitts Creek at Folck's Mill. General Benjamin Franklin Kelley had put his troops, mostly untested "100 day" soldiers, in a defensive line three miles northeast of town to protect the bridge over the Baltimore Pike (now U.S. 40/I-68). The green Union troops held their ground, repulsing the Confederate attacks.

The Confederates retreated at night to Oldtown, where they recrossed the Potomac after capturing the small garrison.

Confederate Jesse McNeil's Rangers captured Generals Kelley and George Crook at the Barnum Hotel in Cumberland in a daring nighttime raid on February 21, 1865. Both officers were soon exchanged.

*How to get there: Cumberland is nearly three hours northwest of Washington, D.C. Take Interstate 270 to I-70 to I-68 West.*

# OLDTOWN

Pioneer Thomas Cresap established an Indian trading post called King Opessa's Town, named after a Shawnee chief, in 1741. The settlement was located near the juncture of the North and South Branches of the Potomac. Cresap was an early promoter of trade with the Indians and, along with George Washington, championed development up the river. Washington visited Cresap numerous times. The post later became Oldtown.

Cresap's youngest son, Michael, built a house in Oldtown in 1764 that is the oldest surviving building in Allegany County, Maryland. Michael led a company of Maryland soldiers to the siege of Boston in 1775, but he got sick and attempted to return home. He died in New York City.

Oldtown was the site of a Civil War skirmish on August 2, 1864. After retreating from their repulse at Folck's Mill, Confederate cavalry under John McCausland sought to cross the Potomac, only to find a Union regiment under Colonel Israel Stough blocking the way on Alum Hill, between the

Michael Cresap, son of legendary frontiersman Thomas Cresap, built the oldest surviving building in Allegany County, Maryland, in 1764. *Garrett Peck.*

Potomac and C&O Canal Locks 69 and 70. The Confederates outflanked the position along the towpath, and the Union troops retreated across the river to a blockhouse with an armored B&O Railroad train at their disposal. Confederate artillery knocked out the train's engine, and many of the Federal troops fled into the woods. Surrounded in the blockhouse, Stough surrendered with eighty of his men.

Five days later, Union general William Averell caught up with the Confederate cavalry at Moorefield, West Virginia. A dawn attack shattered the Rebels and provided significant prisoners, wrecking the Confederate cavalry for the upcoming Shenandoah Valley Campaign.

*How to get there: Oldtown is about twelve miles west of Paw Paw, or fifteen miles east of Cumberland, on Maryland State Route 51.*

# Paw Paw Tunnel

The town of Paw Paw, West Virginia, is named after the tree, and it also gives name to the C&O Canal tunnel nearby. It took twelve years (1836–48) to blast the 3,118-foot-long tunnel through the mountain to avoid the six-mile Paw Paw Bends in the river—and it nearly bankrupted the canal. The Paw Paw Tunnel is one of the most interesting things to see along the Potomac. It is an easy walk, one that requires only enough stamina to conquer one's fear of the dark.

The walk to the tunnel begins along the towpath, which has a railing inside the tunnel to prevent people from falling in the water. *If you don't have a*

An engineering marvel, the Paw Paw Tunnel took twelve years to build and nearly bankrupted the C&O Canal. *Library of Congress.*

*flashlight, don't even think about entering the tunnel!* It is pitch black once you move beyond the entrance. The far end is a tiny point of light more than half a mile away.

After you emerge from the tunnel on the north side, continue another half a mile along the towpath. Take the fire trail on your right; this is the Tunnel Hill Trail, which takes you over the mountain. It is a somewhat strenuous hike, rising several hundred feet via switchbacks to the summit and then descending the mountain. Soon you will see a spectacular curve of the Potomac below. The trail offers interpretive markers, as German and Irish workers lived along the path during the tunnel's construction. You end at the south entrance to the Paw Paw Tunnel after a four-mile round trip.

*How to get there: Take Route 9 west of Berkeley Springs, West Virginia, for twenty-five miles through the scenic Cacapon River Valley. Pass through the town of Paw Paw, cross the Potomac on Route 51 and drive half a mile until you see the signs for the tunnel on the right.*

## LITTLE ORLEANS

"Little" is an appropriate name for Orleans. There isn't much to this rough town, but it is an outdoorsman's paradise and gateway to Green Ridge State Park. The area is rugged and isolated; the Potomac is windy but flat. The Fifteen Mile Creek Aqueduct lifts the C&O Canal over the creek in a single arch. Fifteen Mile Creek is popular for canoeing, fishing and inner tubing. George Washington passed through many times, and President Herbert Hoover liked to fish below Little Orleans. On a hill opposite the town is the red brick St. Patrick's Catholic Church, built in 1860 for the Irish working on the C&O Canal. It has a distinct cloverleaf window.

*How to get there: From Hancock, Maryland, drive I-68 West for ten miles and then go south on Orleans Road for six miles.*

## SIDELING HILL ROAD CUT

Interstate 68 was built in the 1980s to connect western Maryland to Ohio. Before then, motorists used U.S. 40, which traversed Sideling Hill with a hairpin curve at the summit. Because of the high automobile accident rate, planners opted to cut the interstate directly into the 1,600-foot-high ridgeline.

The road cut for the new interstate highway was begun in 1983 and completed sixteen months later. Some ten million tons of rock were excavated to create the 340-foot-deep road cut. This is perhaps the single best place to see how the geology of the Potomac River formed in what is now the Valley and Ridge Province.

The rock of Sideling Hill formed over a 25-million-year period—from 365 to 340 million years ago during the Mississippian period of the middle Paleozoic era. The sedimentary layers were once part of a river delta near sea level and then later a swamp. The oldest rock is on the bottom, the youngest on top.

About 250 million years ago, the North American and African tectonic plates collided to form the supercontinent Pangaea. The intense pressure compressed the land and pushed it upward into a series of parallel ridges, the Allegheny Mountains. The layers of sedimentary rock were squeezed into a "syncline," a U-shaped fold. Shale once covered the mountain, but it eroded to form the valleys on either side. Sandstone at the top of the ridge resists erosion, protecting the layers below it.

*How to get there: The Sideling Hill Road Cut is six miles west of Hancock, Maryland, on Interstate 68.*

# THE COLONIAL FRONTIER

The colonial frontier along the Potomac ran beyond the Blue Ridge Mountains. Indians hunted in the woods, German and Irish settlers built small farms and the colonial elite came to take the healing waters at a spring. These clashed in the French and Indian War starting in 1755 as the frontier rolled back temporarily. Maryland built Fort Frederick to protect its settlers, while George Washington built a chain of forts along the mountains. The French defeat in the war reopened the frontier to settlers, and the Indians were pushed beyond the Ohio River.

In the nineteenth century, the C&O Canal unlocked the region to commerce, development and industry. Two major inland ports took shape to support the canal and canawlers: Hancock and Williamsburg. Both would see considerable action during the Civil War as Confederates targeted the canal.

## BERKELEY SPRINGS

Officially known as Bath—but more commonly called Berkeley Springs—this town is the country's first spa resort and one of the most interesting towns in the West Virginia Panhandle. A long, steep ridgeline of Tuscarora sandstone parallels the town to the west, and this mountain, Warm Springs Ridge, is the source for the town's mineral waters.

Indians came to the healing waters from as far north as Canada and as far south as the Carolinas. When settlers began streaming south from

Pennsylvania into the Shenandoah Valley in 1730, they learned of the springs as well.

In 1748, Colonel William Fairfax, cousin to Lord Thomas Fairfax and manager of Fairfax's vast Northern Neck estate, sent surveying parties to mark tracts of land for sale. One of the men he hired was the sixteen-year-old George Washington. The teenager stopped to take the "Medicinal Springs" marked on a map the year before by Thomas Jefferson's father. The springs were already well known, as attested by the young Washington's diary entry: "March 18th, 1748, We this day called to see Ye Fam'd Warm Springs." Bathing was outside; the bathing pools were simply dug into the ground and hidden by brush screens. The colony's well-to-do brought their families to take the waters, which flow at a constant 74.3 degrees at two thousand gallons per minute out of five major springs.

Bath was considered an immoral place by religious authorities, as there was gambling and horse racing. None of this seemed to bother George Washington, who returned many times and bought substantial property in the area. In 1749, William Fairfax hired Washington as assistant surveyor to lay out the city of Alexandria. Impressed by what he had seen, Washington used his income to buy 1,500 acres in the Shenandoah Valley—the first of many land purchases he would make in the region. He was on his way to establishing himself among the Virginia colony's gentry.

In 1776, Lord Fairfax granted fifty acres to Virginia to develop a bath resort. Later that year, Virginia offered the land for sale in 131 lots, with the mineral springs at the center. The purchasers included many of Virginia's elite, such as George Washington and three signers of the Declaration of Independence. The founders created a British-style grid and named the town Bath after the more famous town in England. The main street (north–south) later became Washington Street.

Innkeeper and inventor James Rumsey met George Washington in Bath on Washington's trip west in 1784. The general was impressed with Rumsey's inventions and so appointed him to be the first engineer of the Potowmack Company. Frustrated with the slow progress, Rumsey resigned in 1786 to work on a new invention: a steamboat, which he tested the following year in Shepherdstown.

Rumsey built the first bathhouse in 1784, so that bathing no longer needed to be outside. That same year, George Washington completed a house in town. The Roman Bath House was constructed in 1815, and the Main Bathhouse was added in 1929. Both are part of Berkeley Springs State Park, which at just seven acres is one of the country's smallest state parks.

Visitors can walk among the springs and see Washington's stone bath from 1748. Water is free from the public tap by the Roman Bath House—bring cartons to fill or buy them from the park.

For a massage and bath, reservations are highly recommended, especially on weekends. The state park facilities are austere (can you say Soviet-era?). Prices are very reasonable and usually consist of a bath, shower and massage (half-hour or full hour). There are numerous private spas in town as well.

Berkeley Springs has a thriving arts community and a good restaurant scene—this is a resort town, after all. Other sites to see include Berkeley Castle, built in 1885. It overlooks the state park on State Route 9 on the steep Warm Springs Ridge above and is open for tours. Also nearby is Cacapon State Park and the Coolfont Resort.

Whatever you do, do not miss the Prospect Peak Scenic Overlook, three miles west of Berkeley Springs on State Route 9. This was one of George Washington's favorite views, and you can see why. Below is a stunning view of the Potomac River, along with Great Cacapon village and the B&O Railroad.

*How to get there: Berkeley Springs is two hours west of Washington, D.C. From the Beltway, take Interstate 270 North, then I-70 West. Exit at U.S. 522 South at Hancock, Maryland, and proceed five miles to the town.*

# HANCOCK

Hancock is the narrowest point in the state of Maryland, barely two miles wide, and it likewise marks the northernmost point on the Potomac. It is named after Edward Joseph Hancock Jr., who operated a ferry. It was the site of a small blockhouse built in 1755, Fort Tonoloway, to protect frontier Maryland from Indian attacks. A year later, the line of defense shifted east to Fort Frederick after Braddock's defeat at Fort Duquesne.

Hancock became a port when the C&O Canal arrived in 1839, and there you'll see the Tonoloway Creek Aqueduct (a single-arch aqueduct), Lock 52 and the adjacent Hancock C&O Canal Museum. The canal also drew Confederate attention during the Civil War. On January 5–6, 1862, Confederate general "Stonewall" Jackson shelled Hancock from the opposite shore after the town refused to surrender. His men burned the B&O Railroad bridge at Great Cacapon, and Jackson then retreated.

Today, Hancock is a gateway to exploring the C&O Canal and the Western Maryland Rail Trail. The latter is a paved bicycle trail that was once a railroad track, the Western Maryland Railroad, which reached Hancock in 1905. The trail is twenty-three miles long (one way), beginning (or ending) at Big Pool near Fort Frederick, passing through Hancock at the ten-mile point and continuing on to Pearre, opposite Great Cacapon. As it is paved, the WMRT can be a nice alternative to cycling the often-muddy C&O towpath.

## *Round Top Cement Mill*

Three miles upriver from Hancock are the ruins of the Round Top Cement Mill, which opened in 1838 and supplied much of the cement for the western portion of the C&O Canal, the U.S. Capitol and the Washington Monument. Round Top is a distinctly conical mountain west of Hancock; this limestone-rich mountain provided raw materials for the cement mill. Eight kilns produced up to forty-eight tons of burnt lime cement each day. The cement mill had trouble competing against Portland cement, and after a major fire in 1903, it was closed for good. The ruins of the cement mill are squeezed between the C&O Canal and the Western Maryland Rail Trail. The kilns still exist, as does its brick smokestack; gone is its water wheel that drew power from the canal. Two hundreds yards east of the mill is a fascinating natural feature: Devil's Eyebrow, a limestone cave protected by layers of sandstone, shale and siltstone that give it an "eyebrow."

*How to get there: Hancock is two hours west of Washington, D.C. From the Beltway, take Interstate 270 North and then I-70 West.*

The Round Top Cement Mill near Hancock, Maryland, provided cement for the C&O Canal and public buildings in Washington, D.C. *Garrett Peck.*

# FORT FREDERICK STATE PARK

After the disastrous battle at Fort Duquesne during the French and Indian War, Maryland governor Horatio Sharpe ordered a stone fortress built in 1756 to defend against Indian attacks. It was named after Frederick Calvert, Sixth Lord Baltimore. It was never attacked. British and Hessian prisoners of war were held there during the Revolution. During the Civil War, Union troops garrisoned there protected the C&O Canal and B&O Railroad from Confederate attacks. Today, Fort Frederick is a well-preserved stone fort with bastions at each corner and two restored barracks. The state park contains 585 acres. Summertime visitors can watch historians re-create 1750s life.

Fort Frederick State Park is located near Big Pool, a natural basin along the C&O Canal, which also marks the beginning of the Western Maryland Rail Trail. Four miles upriver from the fort is the Licking Creek Aqueduct, at ninety feet the largest single-arch span on the C&O.

Two miles downstream from Fort Frederick is McCoy's Ford. After the Battle of Antietam, Confederate general J.E.B. Stuart led 1,800 cavalrymen across the Potomac there on October 10, 1862, and began a harrying ride around the Union Army of the Potomac that led him to Chambersburg, Pennsylvania. He narrowly escaped, recrossing the river at White's Ford near Leesburg.

Three miles downstream from Fort Frederick are the "Four Locks" of the C&O Canal (Locks 47 through 50). These lifted the canal across the base of the Neck, bypassing a long loop in the river.

*How to get there: Fort Frederick is one mile off Interstate 70, Exit 12 (Big Pool), and is eighteen miles west of Hagerstown, Maryland.*

# WILLIAMSPORT

Otho Holland Williams, a Revolutionary War general, founded Williamsport in 1787 at the juncture of Conococheague Creek and the Potomac. It was located along the Indian trading routes, and a ferry to Virginia had existed there since 1775.

The largest surviving Indian fish trap is located below Williamsport, and it spans the width of the river. A fish trap was built by placing large stones to form a giant letter "V," with the apex facing downstream. The fish would get caught in the trap, and the current would prevent them from escaping. Fish traps like this were a major hindrance to navigation, and as president of the Potowmack Company, George Washington ordered them demolished. A freed slave named George Pointer was sent to do the dirty work. In September 1789, he reported that his crew had destroyed forty-four traps out of seventy-three that they found. The Williamsport fish trap can be seen just upriver from the Interstate 81 bridge.

Washington considered Williamsport as a site for the new nation's capital, but he rejected it for its geographic isolation. The rapids in the river made it difficult to reach; the Potowmack Company later built a skirting canal around Williamsport.

Williamsport was one of the major service communities for the C&O Canal, which came to the town in 1834. It was a canal town in every sense of the word. Williamsport marks the near halfway point along the canal between Georgetown and Cumberland. The three-span, 210-foot Conococheague Aqueduct lifts the canal over the creek.

Williamsport is rich in transportation history, as a one-mile round-trip walk along the towpath from Conococheague Aqueduct and Cushwa Basin to Lock 44 shows. The canal is watered along this stretch. Cushwa Basin was one of the turning basins for canalboats, drawing its name from Cushwa Warehouse, a building that predates the canal and is now the C&O Canal Visitor Center. Next to it is a trolley barn power station, built in 1896. The Western Maryland Railroad built a unique lift bridge over the canal in 1923 to let boats pass underneath. Unfortunately, the great flood closed the canal for good the following year. Nearby is a Bollman bridge, built in 1879 to carry light traffic over the canal.

The Valley Turnpike (macadamized road)—now U.S. 11—extended up the Shenandoah River Valley, connecting Williamsport to Staunton. Chartered in 1834 by the Virginia legislature, it was completed in 1840 and brought agricultural goods out of the valley, where they were loaded on canalboats and shipped downriver. Coal was also shipped from Williamsport.

After the defeat at Gettysburg in July 1863, Robert E. Lee's Army of Northern Virginia found itself trapped along the Potomac by raging floodwaters that followed days of torrential downpours. Union cavalry had destroyed the Confederate pontoon bridge, and while engineers worked to build a new one, the trapped army dug a line of trenches stretching from Williamsport to Falling Waters three miles downriver. Complicating the situation were thousands of casualties from the battle, who turned Williamsport into a giant hospital. The Confederates dismantled Williamsport warehouses to build a makeshift bridge at Falling Waters. One corps finally forded the Potomac at Williamsport, while the other two corps retreated at Falling Waters on the night of July 13–14. Abutments from a stone bridge still stand at the Falling Waters crossing site.

*How to get there: Williamsport is at the intersection of Interstates 70 and 81, six miles south of Hagerstown, Maryland.*

# ANTIETAM

## *The Bloodiest Day*

Fought on September 17, 1862, the Battle of Antietam was the bloodiest day in American history. About 23,110 men were casualties in the terrible carnage—and of these, nearly 6,500 died. Many were buried in Antietam National Cemetery. The battle is named after Antietam Creek, a cool, spring-fed stream that originates in Pennsylvania and then courses south to join the Potomac.

After his victory at Second Manassas in August 1862, Confederate general Robert E. Lee invaded Maryland via White's Ford. Needing to open a supply line to the Shenandoah Valley, Lee divided his army into four detachments, sending three under Stonewall Jackson to surround the 12,500-man Federal garrison at Harpers Ferry. Lee sent the fourth detachment to Hagerstown to guard the South Mountain passes.

When Union general George McClellan, commander of the Army of the Potomac, learned of Lee's army's division, he cautiously moved to attack (a soldier had found Lee's orders to divide the army wrapped around three cigars near Frederick, the so-called Lost Order). On September 14, McClellan punched through South Mountain, but rather than pouncing on the retreating Confederates, he waited three days to attack while Lee quickly reassembled his army around Sharpsburg. Lee could have retreated over Pack Horse Ford but instead chose to fight a defensive battle, though he was heavily outnumbered.

Sharpsburg was a farming town founded in 1763. George Washington briefly considered it as a site for the nation's capital. At the time of the battle in 1862, it was a small town of 1,300 people. Four beautiful stone arched bridges built about 1836 cross Antietam Creek. The Upper, Middle and Lower Bridge (also known as the Burnside Bridge, as this is where Burnside's corps crossed) traverse the battlefield. The fourth bridge, near the mouth of Antietam Creek, carries the Harpers Ferry Road over it.

Rather than coordinating the assault, McClellan threw his army into the battle in piecemeal frontal attacks on September 17. Lee improvised and countered every punch. At the end of the day, as Union general Ambrose Burnside's corps threatened to turn his right flank, a Confederate division under A.P. Hill arrived from Harpers Ferry and counterattacked, driving Burnside back. The Confederates held the field, though the casualties on both sides were enormous. Lee retreated to Virginia the following night over Pack Horse Ford, ending the invasion.

Antietam is recognized as one of the turning points in the Civil War. Though a tactical draw, it was a Union strategic victory in that it repelled the Confederate invasion. President Abraham Lincoln was waiting for a battlefield success to issue the Emancipation Proclamation, which freed the slaves in states under rebellion. He issued the proclamation on September 22, five days after Antietam.

President Abraham Lincoln towers over Union general George McClellan and his officers after the Battle of Antietam. *Library of Congress.*

Union general Ambrose Burnside's corps storms the "Burnside Bridge" in a crucial moment during the Battle of Antietam. *Library of Congress.*

As Civil War battlefields go, Antietam National Battlefield is one of the best. It is remarkably well preserved. The National Park Service interpretations are first-class. It can be viewed entirely by car on an eight-mile driving tour, though people are encouraged to walk the terrain on the numerous trails. The battlefield route is ideal for bicyclists, with very light traffic and many places to dismount. Any tour—whether car or bike—should begin at the visitor center. The route then follows the course of the battle as it unfolded—at the Dunker Church and the Cornfield in the north, south to Bloody Lane and, finally, to the Burnside Bridge.

It is particularly moving to see the Sunken Road, a rutted path created by countless wagonloads of farmer's goods driven to market. The Confederates used the road as a makeshift trench, but when the Union troops flanked the position, they fired straight down the road into the enemy ranks. Hundreds of Confederates fell, and the lane filled with dead and wounded. Thus it earned its moniker, Bloody Lane. A stone

A gruesome image of Confederate dead at Antietam, the bloodiest day in American history. *Library of Congress.*

observation tower stands at the end of the Sunken Road; from there you can see almost the entire battlefield.

Every year since 1989, the Memorial Illumination of Antietam National Battlefield is held in December. More than twenty-three thousand candles placed across the battlefield are lit at dusk, representing the dead and wounded soldiers who fought at Antietam.

Some of the local residents from Sharpsburg hid in Killiansburg Cave during the battle. This is right along the riverbank near C&O Canal mile marker 76; it is about a six-mile round-trip walk if you park at Lock 38 near the Ferry Hill house across from Shepherdstown.

## EXPLORING ANTIETAM CREEK

The C&O Canal passes over the creek via the Antietam Creek Aqueduct, and nearby is the beautiful stone bridge that carries Harpers Ferry Road over the creek. The town of Antietam was a small manufacturing site at the mouth of the creek and home to the Antietam Iron Works, which supplied pig iron for the Foxall and, later, Mason foundry in Georgetown. It closed in 1886.

Antietam Creek is wonderful to explore in the summer, either by canoe or by inner tube. The creek is spring-fed, so it is cool. It is two to four feet deep and winds under a thick canopy of trees. There are outfitters in Harpers Ferry and Knoxville, Maryland, who can equip you with a guide, inner tube and lunch.

*How to get there: From Washington, D.C., take Interstate 270 and 70 West. Exit at Alt U.S. 40 West to Boonsboro and follow the signs through Boonsboro to Sharpsburg and Antietam National Battlefield.*

# Dam No. 4

A few miles west of Sharpsburg is Dam No. 4, part of the C&O Canal. It makes a fascinating excursion from Antietam and a lovely drive through the country. The first Dam No. 4 was built from 1832 to 1835 as a rubble structure that floodwaters damaged. The current masonry dam was built in 1856 and stretches eight hundred feet across the river.

Behind Dam No. 4 is the thirteen-mile-long Big Slackwater, a calm reservoir designed for canalboats to traverse, and thus there is a stretch where there is no C&O Canal at all. From the dam, walk a mile upriver to the inlet lock, where boats reentered the canal from the slackwater.

Dam No. 4 Cave is 1.1 miles downriver along the C&O towpath. The stone here is Conococheague limestone, about 470 to 500 million years old, but it eroded into a cave within the last several thousand years. Bring a flashlight to explore the cave.

*How to get there: From Sharpsburg, take Route 65 North and then go west on Taylor's Landing Road. Turn left on Woburn Road and then another left on Dam No. 4 Road.*

# Shepherdstown

Shepherdstown is a small town rich in history and eighteenth- and nineteenth-century architecture, as well as thriving art galleries, college life and restaurant scene. Founded in 1734 as Mecklenburg (note the German influence— Pennsylvania Dutch settled the town), it became Shepherdstown in 1798.

Just downstream (southeast) of town is Pack Horse Ford, also know as Boteler's Ford, Swearingen's Ford and Blackford's Ford. This ford has been used since prehistoric times: it was part of the Indians' "plain path" that followed the migrating buffalo. The Iroquois Confederacy in New York sent war parties down the path to fight its historical enemies, the Cherokees and Catawbas, in the Carolina mountains. Thus a road already existed, and it is no wonder that Shepherdstown became the first incorporated town in what is now West Virginia—it was the first place that settlers from Pennsylvania set foot after crossing the river. During the American Revolution, southern troops marched north on the "Bee Line" that crossed the Potomac at Pack Horse Ford.

Shepherdstown is built on a bluff high above the Potomac. The site was chosen because a small stream provided hydro power to Thomas Shepherd's Mill. At forty feet tall, it is the world's largest working water wheel. It is privately owned and not open for touring.

A seventy-five-foot Ionic granite column on the riverbank, the Rumsey Monument, marks the occasion when James Rumsey took his steamboat for a test run on the Potomac in December 1787, twenty years before Robert Fulton did the same. This offers one of the best views of the river.

The ruins of Boteler's Mill still stand near Pack Horse Ford 1.5 miles east of town; it provided cement for the C&O Canal. C&O boats would leave the canal via a special lock, cross the river to Boteler's Mill and load up there. They would then continue up the canal to construction sites.

Directly across the river is the Ferry Hill plantation. Henry Kyd Douglas grew up there; he enlisted with the Confederates and after the Civil War penned his memoirs, *I Rode with Stonewall*, as he served on Stonewall Jackson's

A view toward Shepherdstown from the James Rumsey Bridge. Confederate troops burned the bridge in 1861, leaving the abutments seen in the foreground. *Garrett Peck.*

staff. The house served as headquarters for the C&O National Park until 2001. Three miles beyond that is Sharpsburg, Maryland, and Antietam National Battlefield.

Swearingen's ferry began operating in 1765 but was later replaced by a toll bridge in 1850. In the summer of 1861, Henry Kyd Douglas's regiment was sent from Harpers Ferry to burn the bridge. He wrote later, "I was with the company that set fire to it, and when, in the glare of the burning timbers, I saw the glowing windows in my home on the hill beyond the river and knew my father was a stockholder in the property I was helping to destroy, I realized that war had begun." The bridge abutments still stand in the river. Douglas was buried at Shepherdstown's Elmwood Cemetery, the final resting spot for 252 Confederates, many of whom died during the Antietam Campaign.

Shepherd University, founded in 1872, is the reason the town thrives today. The college gives the town its nickname, "Georgetown West." Shepherdstown has a quaint historic district along German Street about one-third of a mile long. It sported one of the country's first movie theaters, opened in 1909 and now the Shepherdstown Opera House, an art house cinema. The town also hosts the annual Contemporary American Theater Festival.

*How to get there: Shepherdstown is three miles southwest of Sharpsburg, Maryland, on Route 34.*

## The Battle of Shepherdstown

Pack Horse Ford was a natural route for invasion and retreat during the Civil War. A shallow dam still exists that provided water for Boteler's Mill just above the ford. This was where Robert E. Lee retreated over the Potomac after Antietam in 1862; it was also one of the river crossings that he used to invade the North in 1863 in the Gettysburg Campaign. It was where Jubal Early crossed in his raid on Washington, D.C., in 1864. Pack Horse Ford was also a battlefield on September 19–20, 1862, just two days after Antietam.

The thousands of Confederate wounded from the battles at South Mountain and Antietam were sent across the Potomac to Shepherdstown, where they quickly overwhelmed the town. Lee needed to prevent the Federals from crossing the river while he dealt with the medical tragedy facing his army, so he positioned a rear guard of two brigades and forty-four guns on an eighty-foot bluff on the Virginia side overlooking Pack Horse Ford. This was under his artillery commander, General William Pendleton.

Union artillery and sharpshooters dueled with the Confederates on September 19 from opposite sides of the river. After dark, five hundred Federal infantry crossed the river and surprised the Confederates, taking five guns before retreating. Pendleton panicked, reporting to Lee that he had lost many of his guns. Lee ordered A.P. Hill's division to drive the Federals back.

The Union Fifth Corps commander, General Fitz John Porter, sent three brigades back over the river into Virginia the next morning. A.P. Hill's two thousand men attacked a similar number of Federal troops. Porter quickly ordered a retreat. Though the Confederates came under withering fire from seventy Union artillery pieces across the river, they broke the Federal line. The Union troops fled across the Potomac in panic, many of them drowning. However, the battle deterred Lee from reinvading Maryland, which he had hoped to do after Antietam.

*How to get there: From downtown Shepherdstown, take German Street east. The road becomes Cement Mill Road and leads you to Pack Horse Ford, 1.5 miles east of town. The battlefield is up the hill on Trough Road.*

# Harpers Ferry

Harpers Ferry takes the prize for the most historically interesting place to visit on the Potomac that combines natural beauty and recreation. And it lies only fifty-seven miles upriver from Washington, D.C. Set on a peninsula and surrounded by cliffs, the setting is nothing short of spectacular. Thomas Jefferson agreed, as he wrote after a visit there in 1783:

> *The passage of the Patowmac through the Blue Ridge is perhaps one of the most stupendous scenes in Nature. You stand on a very high point of land. On your right comes up the Shenandoah, having ranged along the foot of the mountain a hundred miles to seek a vent. On your left approaches the Patowmac, in quest of a passage also. In the moment of their junction they rush together against the mountain, rend it asunder and pass off to the sea…This scene is worth a voyage across the Atlantic.*

The view is equally good at the Point, the tip of Harpers Ferry where the Potomac and Shenandoah Rivers converge. It's like Pittsburgh in miniature.

Harpers Ferry offers a chance to see the geologic forces that created such a spectacular setting. Most of the rock is sedimentary shale (phyllite) and sandstone (quartzite). These are more than 500 million years old. When Africa and North America collided 250 million years ago, the land was pushed up; then waters from the Potomac's predecessors eroded it, carving the river valleys and water gap that you see now. The soft phyllite was used throughout Harpers Ferry for steps and walls, while quartzite is more durable and was often used for buildings.

A Pennsylvania Dutchman named Peter Stephens began a ferry over the Potomac in 1733. Robert Harper bought the ferry in 1747, and the town was named after him. Three states come together at this point: Maryland, Virginia and West Virginia. Harpers Ferry is the lowest point in West Virginia, and it frequently floods.

The two rivers provided hydraulic power for this early industrial site. President George Washington created the U.S. Arsenal and Armory at Harpers Ferry in 1796, one of two in the country (the other was in Springfield, Massachusetts). Stretching six hundred yards and including twenty buildings, the armory employed four hundred men and churned out ten thousand weapons each year. The U.S. Arsenal storing the weapons was composed of two buildings near the B&O bridge. Meriwether Lewis (of Lewis and Clark fame) came to Harpers Ferry in March 1803 to purchase weapons and build a boat before setting out to explore the lands of the Louisiana Purchase.

The armories at Harpers Ferry and Springfield produced much of the country's small arms—muskets at first and later rifles. The machinery was so precise that pieces were interchangeable, as was famously demonstrated with ten different muskets at the industrial exhibition in London's Crystal Palace in the 1850s.

In 1836, the ferry was shut down, replaced by a railroad bridge for the B&O designed by Benjamin Latrobe, the architect for the U.S. Capitol. The C&O Canal and the Winchester and Potomac Railroad likewise served the town. By the eve of the Civil War in 1860, Harpers Ferry was an industrial town of three thousand people. It manufactured more than small arms, having a flour mill, a paper mill, a cotton mill and an iron foundry—all along the Shenandoah River on Virginius Island.

# JOHN BROWN'S RAID

"If John Brown did not end the war that ended slavery, he did at least begin the war that ended slavery. If we look over the dates, places, and men, for which this honor is claimed, we shall find that not Carolina, but Virginia—not Fort Sumter, but Harpers Ferry and the arsenal—not Major Anderson, but John Brown, began the war that ended American slavery and made this a free republic," wrote abolitionist and former slave Frederick Douglass about John Brown's raid on Harpers Ferry.

John Brown was a fanatic and a frenzied abolitionist, much like an Old Testament prophet. He believed that slavery could only be overthrown by

*John Brown*

A portrait and signature of radical abolitionist John Brown, who attempted to incite a slave rebellion by seizing the U.S. Arsenal at Harpers Ferry in October 1859. *Library of Congress.*

bloodshed, and thus he is also called the father of American terrorism. Financed by wealthy Northern abolitionists known as the Secret Six, Brown assembled twenty-one followers, including three sons and five African Americans, on the rented Kennedy Farm nearby (2506 Chestnut Grove Road, Keedysville, Maryland). He called his men the Provisional Army of the United States.

Brown believed that if he seized the U.S. Arsenal, he could arm the slaves and start a slave revolt. He began the insurrection at 10:00 p.m. on October 16, 1859. Only one man guarded the armory, which Brown's men easily captured. Thousands of rifles were now in their hands. They took prominent local slaveholders, such as Lewis Washington, as hostages.

Word spread the next day to the local militia, which sprang into action. Rather than fomenting a slave insurrection, Brown faced an angry and armed white mob on the surrounding heights. One group forded the Potomac and seized the railroad bridge, trapping Brown's party. Surrounded by cliffs, Harpers Ferry was indefensible. Frederick Douglass had warned Brown that Harpers Ferry was a "perfect steel trap, and that once in he would never get out alive."

After losing several men, Brown gathered the survivors in the brick engine house. Thirty-seven hours after Brown captured the arsenal, Colonel Robert E. Lee and Lieutenant J.E.B. Stuart led a detachment of ninety U.S. marines from the Washington Navy Yard that stormed the engine house and captured or killed the party. The slave insurrection had failed.

Although Brown had attacked federal property, he was tried in nearby Charles Town by the Commonwealth of Virginia and found guilty of murder, treason and inciting slave insurrection. Brown went to the gallows unrepentant on December 2, riding on his own coffin. As he left the jail, he handed a guard a note that read, "I John Brown am now quite <u>certain</u>

John Brown assembled his followers for the Harpers Ferry raid at the Kennedy Farm five miles north of Harpers Ferry. *Garrett Peck.*

John Brown was trapped in the arsenal's engine house, and when he refused to surrender, U.S. marines stormed the building and captured him. *Library of Congress.*

that the crimes of this <u>guilty,</u> <u>land</u>: will never be purged <u>away</u>; but with Blood. I had <u>as I now think</u>: <u>vainly</u> flattered myself that without <u>very much</u> bloodshed; it might be done."

Frederick Douglass declined to join the raid. He later said about Brown, "His zeal in the cause of my race was far greater than mine—it was as the burning sun to my taper light. I could live for the slave, but he could die for him."

Brown became a national symbol of abolitionism. The South cheered his execution, while in the North he became a martyr. More than any other event, John Brown's raid proved an irreconcilable split between the free-labor North and slaveholding South. Abraham Lincoln was elected to the presidency less than a year later, and the Civil War would soon begin.

Harpers Ferry National Historical Park includes many sites related to the raid. The John Brown Museum details the story of the fiery abolitionist, while John Brown's Fort (the engine house) stands across the street. Also check out the controversial 1931 granite memorial erected by the United Daughters of the Confederacy and dedicated to Hayward Shepherd, a free black railroad porter who was the first victim of the raid.

## HARPERS FERRY IN THE CIVIL WAR

When Abraham Lincoln was elected president a year after John Brown's raid, the Southern states began seceding. South Carolina bombarded Fort Sumter into submission on April 12–13, 1861, and Lincoln called for seventy-five thousand volunteers to quell the insurrection. Virginia had wanted to remain in the Union, but Lincoln's call for volunteers was too much for the state, which seceded on April 17. The next day, Virginia militia seized the U.S. Arsenal at Harpers Ferry; retreating Federal troops torched the buildings, but the militia braved the flames to save the armory's machinery, which was shipped to Richmond. Thomas Jackson was sent to organize the militia into a fighting force; he would soon earn his nickname "Stonewall" at the Battle of Manassas in July, and his brigade became known as the Stonewall Brigade.

Harpers Ferry changed hands eight times during the Civil War. It was a strategic point, given that the Baltimore and Ohio Railroad crossed the Potomac there, and the B&O was vital for east–west communications for the Union. It was so important that when West Virginia seceded from Virginia in 1863 during the war, the three counties of the Panhandle—through which the B&O traversed—were peeled off and given to the new state, though they were economically and geographically part of the Shenandoah Valley.

Harpers Ferry sat astride a natural north–south corridor, and both Union and Confederacy used this to invade. During Confederate general Robert E. Lee's first invasion of the North in September 1862, he sent Stonewall Jackson's corps to capture the 12,500-man Federal garrison at Harpers Ferry and open a supply line to the Shenandoah Valley. Jackson divided his

After Virginia seceded from the Union, Federal soldiers torched the arsenal at Harpers Ferry. Confederates braved the flames to save the machinery. *Library of Congress.*

command into three bodies and then surrounded Harpers Ferry from the high ground on Maryland Heights, Loudoun Heights and School House Ridge, trapping the garrison under Colonel Dixon Miles in the town.

The Union garrison attempted to defend the town from Bolivar Heights, but the men were surrounded. Confederate artillery bombarded them from every direction, and a night attack from the Murphy Farm turned their left flank, making the Federal position untenable. On September 15, the Union garrison at Harpers Ferry surrendered to Jackson's forces. Dixon was killed by an artillery shell moments after he ordered the surrender. This was the largest capitulation of American forces until May 1942, when the U.S. Army surrendered to the Japanese on the Bataan Peninsula in the Philippines. Jackson then joined Lee at Sharpsburg in time for the bloody Battle of Antietam. One division, that of A.P. Hill, stayed behind to parole the prisoners and then hustled up to stave off defeat for the Confederates.

After Antietam, the Union Army of the Potomac reoccupied Harpers Ferry. It improved the fortifications around the town, building Fort Duncan west of Maryland Heights. Harpers Ferry would always be an inviting target. On the night of January 9–10, 1864, Confederate guerrilla leader John Mosby attacked a Federal position held by Major Henry Cole on Loudoun Heights in the bitter cold and was repulsed. This was the first time Federal troops bested Mosby.

Harpers Ferry changed hands eight times during the Civil War. Its bridges were destroyed and industry demolished. The town never fully recovered. *Library of Congress.*

In August 1864, Union general Philip Sheridan made Harpers Ferry his headquarters as he prepared to invade the Shenandoah Valley. He further entrenched Bolivar Heights to protect his supply line. After defeating the Confederates in three major pitched battles, he burned most of the crops in the valley, depriving the Confederacy of a major source of food.

Harpers Ferry never recovered from the Civil War. The armory and arsenal were destroyed, and the population dwindled to one hundred people. Though new industries were built to replace it, the floods of 1870 and 1889 devastated much of the industry along Virginius Island. Stone abutments from several bridges that no longer exist still stand in the river; they were destroyed in the Civil War or by floodwaters.

Storer College was founded in Harpers Ferry in 1867 in Upper Town to educate freed slaves. The Niagara Movement, led by W.E.B. Du Bois, first met there in 1906. A year after the U.S. Supreme Court ended segregation in *Brown v. Board of Education* in 1954, the college was closed.

# EXPLORING HARPERS FERRY

Harpers Ferry National Historical Park came into existence in 1944 and comprises 2,300 of the most historically significant acres in the United States. It includes much of Lower Town, the ruins of industrial facilities on Virginius Island, Maryland Heights, Bolivar Heights and more. Parking is available at the visitor center. Take the shuttle bus to downtown and then start at the Point.

There are really two towns—the historic Lower Town (now part of the National Park Service), which floods often, and the newer Upper Town, safely built atop Camp Hill. Restaurants are on High and Potomac Streets in Lower Town. Much of the town is a museum with many different exhibits to explore on town life, industry, John Brown, the Civil War, natural history and African American history.

The Appalachian Trail passes through Harpers Ferry. It winds down South Mountain, Maryland, and then follows the C&O Canal towpath to the west. A footbridge was added to the railroad bridge in 1985, and the trail crosses the Potomac there. It passes through the town, up to Jefferson Rock and then crosses the Shenandoah River into Virginia.

## Cliff Trail (Jefferson Rock Trail) to Storer College

The shortest hike in Harpers Ferry may only take you five minutes to reach the destination. From the riverfront, climb forty-four steps carved into the cliff and past St. Peter's Roman Catholic Church (built in 1833 for the Irish who worked on the C&O Canal and B&O Railroad) to Jefferson Rock overlooking the Shenandoah River. The rock is supported by four sandstone pillars to prevent it from falling and is named after Thomas Jefferson. The view is stunning: this is a great place to see the trees changing colors in the fall. From there you can return down the stairs or continue on to Harper Cemetery and Storer College in Upper Town.

## Bolivar Heights Trail

Bolivar Heights (it rhymes with "Oliver") cuts across the base of the Harpers Ferry peninsula, and it was the key to the Union defenses in the 1862 siege. The Confederate siege lines were several hundred yards to the west on School House Ridge. The Bolivar Heights trail tours the Union lines in a

Jefferson Rock at Harpers Ferry offers a view so profound that Thomas Jefferson described it as "worth a voyage across the Atlantic." *Library of Congress.*

0.6-mile round trip, paralleling a trench line and ending at a Union redoubt dug in 1864. From Bolivar Heights, you can also take the 1.6-mile School House Ridge trail loop to visit the Confederate lines.

## Virginius Island Trail

The Virginius Island trail is a 1.25-mile loop that passes through the remains of industrial sites along the Shenandoah River. The Potowmack Company dug the Shenandoah Canal in 1806 to improve navigation. Later came water tunnels to power the island's industries. You will pass a cotton mill, a paper mill that operated until 1935 and Hall's Rife Works, seized by John Brown during his raid. Still used today, the Winchester and Potomac Railroad opened in 1836 and cuts through the island.

## Maryland Heights Trail

The Maryland Heights Trail provides a tremendous view of Harpers Ferry. You start at the Point, where the Potomac and Shenandoah Rivers meet. Continue on to the footbridge over the Potomac to the Maryland side. To your left are the rapids known as the Needles. On your right are foundation ruins of the old railroad bridge, destroyed nine times during the Civil War and swept away by the flood of 1936. When you reach the Maryland side, turn left and walk half a mile past C&O Canal Locks 33 and 34 to the beginning of the Maryland Heights Trail.

Hikers have a choice of two trails on Maryland Heights: the shorter trail to Overlook Cliff (2.8 miles round trip from the trailhead) or the longer loop to the Stone Fort (6.9 miles). The latter also ends at the Overlook Cliff. The hike uphill is moderately strenuous.

The shorter trail climbs Maryland Heights, traverses the top of the ridge and then drops sharply down to Overlook Cliff. It passes a Naval Battery, erected in May 1862 with three heavy Dahlgren guns to protect Maryland from Stonewall Jackson's army during the Shenandoah Valley Campaign. Overlook Hill is the final stop on the hike; the view is 850 feet directly above Harpers Ferry. To return to Harpers Ferry, simply retrace your steps.

The longer Stone Fort trail follows the initial path up Maryland Heights. After one mile, it veers to the left, taking a 4.1-mile loop farther up the heights. This passes several areas of Civil War interest: charcoal making, campgrounds and the Stone Fort. After the Stone Fort, the trail veers south and continues directly to Overlook Cliff. It first passes a one-hundred-pounder battery and then a thirty-pounder battery. The trail then drops steeply down to the Overlook Cliff view.

## DAM NO. 3 AND FORT DUNCAN

Cross the river just like you're going to Maryland Heights, only you continue along the C&O towpath past Byrnes Island to Dam No. 3, about 1.5 miles. The dam provided water to the canal. Nearby are Locks 35 and 36, and directly uphill is Fort Duncan, a Civil War fort built after the Battle of Antietam to protect Harpers Ferry. The hike along the towpath is completely flat, ideal for bikers, casual walkers or even those with baby strollers.

## OTHER RECREATION OPTIONS

For cyclists, the C&O Canal towpath from Harpers Ferry to Shepherdstown and back is about a twenty-four-mile round trip. River rafting and inner tubing are popular in summer on the Shenandoah River. There are several outfitter companies at Harpers Ferry that will take rafters on the river for the day.

*How to get there: Harpers Ferry is fifty-seven miles upriver from Washington, D.C. Take Interstate 270 toward Frederick and merge with I-70 toward Hagerstown, then take U.S. 340 West toward Charles Town. Alternatively, Amtrak connects directly from Washington to Harpers Ferry.*

# The Piedmont

The Piedmont offers beautiful geography of rolling hillsides in both Maryland and Virginia, the dividing zone between the Blue Ridge Mountains and the coastal plane. In Maryland, the Potomac flows through largely rural parts of Frederick and Montgomery Counties, though both counties have become bedroom communities and Washington suburbs. Montgomery County has carefully managed its land, zoning the eastern half for urban density while keeping the western half farmland, preventing sprawl from encroaching. In 1981, the county created an agricultural reserve, showing tremendous foresight, as its population has since boomed.

The Virginia Piedmont of Fairfax, Fauquier and Loudoun Counties had numerous plantations and was sympathetic to the Confederacy during the Civil War. Confederate armies traversed this region three times invading the North, and Union armies traversed it countless times. Confederates under John Singleton Mosby (the "Gray Ghost") and Elijah White formed guerrilla bands to attack Union supply lines. This gave the region its nickname: Mosby's Confederacy. By the end of the war, the bitter divisions and constant fighting had destroyed much of the local economy. The Mosby Heritage Area was created in 1995 in Virginia.

Today, the Piedmont is disappearing under the ever-encroaching suburbs. Scenic farmland is disappearing as strip malls and subdivisions consume the countryside. Yet small farms still exist, as do many wineries. The town of Leesburg has kept its historic charm. Goose Creek, a major Potomac tributary through Loudoun County, is largely pristine.

# BRUNSWICK

Brunswick began as a ferry crossing in 1741. It was a small town along the C&O Canal known as Barry or Berlin until 1890, when the B&O Railroad moved its train yard from Martinsburg, West Virginia. The railroad had taken over the canal the year before after a massive flood shut down the canal and sent it into bankruptcy. Renamed Brunswick, the town grew with the railroad. The rail yards are some of the largest in the world. The B&O was later absorbed into CSX, and most of the rail operations were moved elsewhere. Today, Brunswick is a bedroom community for rail commuters to Washington.

The Brunswick Railroad Museum and C&O Canal Visitor Center sit side by side, reflecting the dual transportation ventures in the town. Lock 30 of the C&O is near downtown Brunswick, right below the Route 17/287 bridge over the Potomac. It was originally made of Seneca red sandstone.

*How to get there: Brunswick is just off U.S. 340, fifteen miles southwest of Frederick, Maryland.*

# POINT OF ROCKS

Point of Rocks overlooks a water gap where the Potomac passes through Catoctin Mountain. By 1690, it had become a major trading point between Indians and colonists. This site was the main point of contention between the B&O Railroad and the C&O Canal. Both wanted the right-of-way in the narrow river embankment. The B&O filed suit in 1828, holding up the C&O for four years before the canal successfully won its case. During the Antietam Campaign, the Confederates damaged C&O Lock 28, a mile upriver, after failing to blow up the Monocacy Aqueduct.

There isn't much to the town, but the railroad station is quaint. The town and U.S. 15 bridge offer excellent views of the Potomac. Many people gather under the bridge in summer to wade and kayak. The river is quite shallow and wide. Opposite Point of Rocks is the Heaters Island Wildlife Management Area. Originally named Conoy Island after an Indian tribe, this wildlife preserve is accessible by boat only.

*How to get there: Point of Rocks is on U.S. Route 15, twelve miles north of Leesburg and thirteen miles south of Frederick.*

# Monocacy Aqueduct

The most beautiful structure on the C&O Canal is the Monocacy Aqueduct, which carries the canal over the Monocacy River. The 516-foot-long, seven-spanned aqueduct was completed in 1833 after four years of construction. It is a marvel. In the center is a raised capstone with the names of the engineers who proudly worked on the structure. The stone was quarried from Sugarloaf Mountain nearby, which at 1,282 feet stands out dramatically.

During the Antietam Campaign, the Confederates attempted to blow up the Monocacy Aqueduct, but the span proved too strong. They damaged Lock 28 instead, just beyond Point of Rocks. Downriver 0.75 miles from the aqueduct is Lock 27, built using Seneca red sandstone. Monocacy Aqueduct gradually deteriorated after the C&O closed in 1924. The flood of 1996 caused especially heavy damage, raising awareness of the need to restore the historic structure. A full restoration was completed in 2005. Today, the Monocacy River is the single largest source of sediment in the Potomac.

*How to get there: Monocacy Aqueduct is forty miles northwest of Washington, D.C. Exit Interstate 495 at River Road and proceed west ten miles and then north on Esworthy Road and Seneca Road; then head west on Darnestown Road to Dickerson. In the town Dickerson, turn left on Mouth of Monocacy Road.*

# White's Ford

On September 4, 1862, Confederate general Robert E. Lee and the Army of Northern Virginia crossed the Potomac at White's Ford on the first invasion of the North that would culminate in the Battle of Antietam. You can see the ford site in Dickerson Conservation Park. (This is not to be confused with White's Ferry, which is several miles south.) Confederate general Jubal Early also crossed at White's Ford on his retreat from the raid on Washington, D.C., in July 1864. Less than half a mile north is Lock 26 on the C&O Canal, widened in the 1870s to allow two boats to pass and made from Seneca red sandstone. A 0.7-mile walk downriver from White's Ford leads you to the marble quarry, used by Benjamin Latrobe to help rebuild Washington after the War of 1812.

*How to get there: White's Ford is in Dickerson Conservation Park off Martinsburg Road. Park at the lot near Lock 26.*

Confederate soldiers ford the Potomac at White's Ford in the first invasion of the North that would conclude with the Battle of Antietam. *Library of Congress.*

## WHITE'S FERRY

The last operating river ferry on the Potomac, White's Ferry is just north of Leesburg, Virginia. After the Civil War, a Confederate cavalry colonel and guerrilla commander, Elijah Veirs White, ran the ferry on his boat, the *General Jubal Early*. White had fought at Ball's Bluff and later organized a Confederate guerrilla unit known as White's Comanches. At the White's Ferry Store and Grill in Maryland, you'll see markers noting the height of the various floods. The 1996 flood came nearly to the top of the second story. Just beyond the ferry is an old iron bridge crossing over the C&O Canal's now dry bed, as well as several culverts. The bridge's footings are Seneca red sandstone.

*How to get there: From downtown Leesburg, take U.S. Route 15 north two miles and then head right on White's Ferry Road.*

# BALL'S BLUFF

Just east of Leesburg was the site of a small but horrific battle early in the Civil War, the Battle of Ball's Bluff. It is now Ball's Bluff Battlefield Regional Park. On October 21, 1861, Union forces crossed the Potomac at Harrison's Island, just south of White's Ferry. Faulty reconnaissance had identified a copse of trees as a Confederate camp. Brigadier General Charles Stone sent across a 1,700-man brigade under Colonel (and senator from Oregon) Edward Baker.

Baker ferried his men over the Potomac and Harrison Island and advanced inland a short distance. An equal number of Confederates under Brigadier General Nathan "Shanks" Evans—one of the heroes of First Manassas in July—repulsed the Federals around the Jackson House. They then counterattacked, driving the Union soldiers down the one-hundred-foot bluff, inflicting frightful casualties and taking more than 550 prisoners. Baker was killed in the debacle that destroyed more than half of his command. He was the only U.S. senator ever killed in battle (he is buried at Congressional Cemetery). Among the wounded was Lieutenant Oliver Wendell Holmes Jr., who would later serve on the U.S. Supreme Court as the "Great Dissenter."

Congress established the Joint Committee on the Conduct of the War after the battle, which then scapegoated General Stone for the defeat. He was arrested and imprisoned for six months, although no charges were filed against him.

Ball's Bluff has numerous hiking paths through it. The main path through the battlefield, including interpretive signs, is a 1.6-mile loop from the parking lot. In the center of the battlefield is the small Ball's Bluff National Cemetery, established in 1865 with the remains of fifty-four Union soldiers, all but one unknown. The red sandstone walls, erected in 1901, were quarried on site. A mile south is Red Rock Wilderness Overlook Regional Park, a sixty-seven-acre park with farm buildings dating from the 1880s, hiking trails and views of the river.

*How to get there: Take Route 7 West to Leesburg and then the Route 15 bypass north. Take a right on Battlefield Parkway and then a left on Ball's Bluff Road.*

# EDWARDS FERRY

Edwards Ferry was a historical ferry over the Potomac. On June 25 and 26, 1863, the Union Army of the Potomac crossed the river there, heading north to shield the cities of the eastern seaboard from Robert E. Lee's Army of Northern Virginia. The two armies would clash just days later at Gettysburg. Two C&O Canal locks are near Edwards Ferry: Lock 25, made from Seneca red sandstone, and the Goose Creek River Lock, designed for canalboats from Goose Creek on the opposite shore to enter the C&O.

*How to get there: From Poolesville, Maryland, drive west on Westerly Road and then south on Edwards Ferry Road.*

# SENECA CREEK

Seneca Creek stretches fourteen miles, and the resulting 6,300-acre Seneca Creek State Park is winding and narrow, reaching far into Montgomery County. The park is a history lover's dream, as a quirk of geology gave the area a natural treasure that was crucial for development along the Potomac: Seneca red sandstone.

Seneca red sandstone was formed in the late Triassic age, 210 to 230 million years ago, in what is now the Piedmont upland. It is a sedimentary rock composed mostly of tiny grains of quartz. Iron oxide gives the rock its unique red color.

Colonials began quarrying red sandstone from the bluffs along the Potomac just west of Seneca Creek. The Potowmack Company employed stone for the Great Falls Skirting Canal locks. The Seneca quarry was instrumental for the C&O Canal, as it provided red sandstone for Locks 8 through 27. Engineers dug a wide turning basin adjacent to the quarry for canalboats to maneuver and anchor. Its walls are lined with Seneca sandstone.

Seneca also has a unique feature that you'll find nowhere else on the C&O: Riley's Lock (Lock 24). It is the only lock that combines both a lock and an aqueduct (Seneca Aqueduct). It's a beautiful structure, once having three red sandstone arches over the creek. A 1971 flood destroyed one of the arches. Next to it is the red sandstone lock keeper's house.

The Seneca stonecutting mill was built in 1837, and you can see its ruins at the end of Tschiffely Mill Road. The mill cut sandstone from the quarry for the upper portion of Cabin John Bridge and, most famously, the Smithsonian Castle (1847). The Seneca quarry, which is behind the mill in the impenetrable, overgrown forest, ceased operations in 1900. The best way to access it is to walk west on the towpath to the end of the holding basin, a quarter mile, then walk due north toward the cliff (assuming the

C&O Canal is dry or frozen over). Above you is the restored quarry master's house (16710 River Road, a private residence). You can also visit the Seneca School House Museum (1865) at 16800 River Road. Both buildings were constructed of Seneca red sandstone.

Less than a mile east along the C&O towpath is Violette's Lock (Lock 23), which has two locks: one for canalboats and the other to let river water into the canal. During the Gettysburg Campaign, Confederate general J.E.B. Stuart crossed the Potomac here at Rowser's Ford on June 27, 1863. His cavalrymen turned a boat sideways as a makeshift bridge over the canal and let the water out of the C&O, knocking the canal out of operation for three days.

*How to get there: Seneca Creek is twelve miles west on River Road from Interstate 495. Turn left on Riley's Lock Road and proceed one mile.*

## Blockhouse Point Conservation Park

Blockhouse Point is a 630-acre Maryland state park that abuts the C&O Canal to the north. Now covered in second-growth forest, the area is woodsy and shaded, making it a pleasant place to hike even on a hot day. There are several observation points atop cliffs with nice views of the canal directly below and the Potomac beyond.

The park gets its name from wooden blockhouses that Union forces built atop the cliffs in 1862. They erected these to protect the C&O Canal and Rowser's Ford from Confederate raids, especially from Colonel John Mosby. Across the river was "Mosby's Confederacy," an area in northern Virginia patrolled by the Confederate guerilla leader to disrupt Union supply lines. During Confederate general Jubal Early's raid on Washington, D.C., in July 1864, the Union troops occupying the blockhouses were pulled back to help defend the nation's capital. Mosby's forces crossed the river and burned three blockhouses, which were never rebuilt.

A 1.5-mile hike leads to Blockhouse Point, and there are numerous hiking trails, including to a spring where Union troops got their water, and to Muddy Branch, site of the main Union encampment.

*How to get there: Blockhouse Point Conservation Park is ten miles west on River Road from Interstate 495.*

# GREAT FALLS

It's hard to believe that a huge waterfall exists so close to Washington, D.C. Great Falls is one of the most spectacular natural sights in our region, and it is incredibly accessible, just fifteen miles upriver. It is a place filled with history, natural beauty and outdoor activities. Great Falls is a keystone sight on the Potomac River.

Great Falls is a seventy-five-foot drop in the Potomac, but rather than a sheer drop, it offers a half-mile jagged cascade that churns and boils the water into a white foam as it plummets between enormous boulders. Just below the falls begins Mather Gorge, named after the first National Park Service director, Stephen Mather.

No two visits to Great Falls are ever the same. Like an impressionist painting, light and water volume are always different. During a drought, the falls slow to a trickle; several days after a major rainstorm, a torrent of water rages through the gorge. Some days it is snowy, while many other days are sunny. In fall, the leaves spectacularly change color.

We view Great Falls as a place of beauty and wonder today, but early settlers saw it as an obstacle. In an era before the internal combustion engine or railroad, how could goods from the mountain get to the Tidewater when there is a huge waterfall in the way? You build a canal around it. In fact, there are two canals on either side of the river: the Potowmack Canal and the C&O Canal.

Great Falls is administered by the National Park Service in two national parks. The Maryland side is part of the C&O Canal Historical Park, while the Virginia side is part of the George Washington Memorial Parkway.

Now then, a word on safety. The waters around Great Falls are some of the most dangerous on the Potomac. *Do not swim or wade in the river.* The river here is quite treacherous, and every year people drown when the current carries them away. Even calm waters are deceptive—below the surface the current is raging. Park rangers are authorized to arrest or ticket people too close to the water. Volunteer kayakers patrol the waters for safety. Since 1991, these trained daredevils hold the Potomac Whitewater Festival, which includes the Great Falls Race down the Class V+ rapids.

## GREAT FALLS: THE VIRGINIA SIDE

The Virginia side of Great Falls is rich in history and natural beauty. Near the main parking lot and visitor center are three overlooks over the falls, often crowded with tourists. The best is Overlook 3, which also has a wooden marker showing the high-water marks for flood years like 1936, 1942 and 1996.

You'll lose most of the people after just a short walk south of the overlooks, which is a pity, as a hike along a winding path—the River Trail—is well worth it. It follows the cliff's edge, where you'll often see rock climbers and kayakers below. Don't miss the "pothole rocks," large holes that the ice age–era river carved. It is easier than the Billy Goat Trails in Maryland, and the many views of Mather Gorge are just as spectacular. At the end, you'll reach the Potowmack Canal.

In 1785, George Washington helped organize the Potowmack Company to bring commerce to the Ohio Country via the Potomac. Great Falls was one of the major obstacles to expanding riverboat traffic, and thus the company built the canal, its most complicated construction project. Washington hired James Rumsey as its superintendent to improve navigation on the river. Rumsey stayed on the job one year and then quit in frustration. He went on to invent the steamboat.

A flood marker shows the Potomac's high-water marks at Great Falls. *Garrett Peck.*

Officially known as the Great Falls Skirting Canal, the Potowmack Canal is more than a mile long and was opened in 1802. It used a series of five locks to lift boats around the waterfall. The locks are partially preserved, but the channel and holding basin silted in. Lock 1 is the most intact. Note the bright red rocks—the locks were built with Seneca red sandstone. The final locks, 4 and 5, are remarkable. They were blasted out of a solid rock wall to raise boats thirty-eight feet. The Canal Cut is a good place to bound up the boulders to view the river below.

Engineers blasted this cut to build locks for the Potowmack Canal, which skirts around Great Falls. *Garrett Peck.*

You can return to the visitor center via the Potowmack Canal Trail. A small town, Matildaville, once existed along the canal's holding basin, providing supplies for the canawlers and workers to man the locks. It was financed by Henry "Light Horse Harry" Lee, who owned the land around Great Falls and who named the town after his wife (Robert E. Lee's mother). The town died when the C&O Canal began operations on the Maryland side of Great Falls in 1828.

If you're in the mood for a longer hike, you can park upriver at Riverbend Park and hike down the Potomac Heritage Trail, which leads to the River Trail. This option offers a 2.5-mile interpretive trail, plus another half-mile to reach the Canal Cut, and thus is a six-mile round trip. Pack a lunch.

*How to get there: From Washington, D.C., take Interstate 495 (the Capitol Beltway) to Georgetown Pike west. Turn right on Old Dominion Drive and follow the signs to Great Falls.*

# GREAT FALLS: THE MARYLAND SIDE

The Maryland side of Great Falls has more hiking choices than the Virginia side. I've outlined the major trails and suggested several hiking possibilities; however, you can also mix and match the trails, depending on your interest.

First, you must choose a place to park your car. The obvious choice is to park at the visitor center, where there is an entrance fee. Now the visitor center, also called Great Falls Tavern, was once a working canal house for families who tended the locks. Nearby is the Washington Aqueduct Dam, which stretches across the river. This provides much of the fresh water for the Washington metropolitan area. Canalboat rides on the *Charles F. Mercer* are offered at Great Falls from April to October, beginning at the visitor center. These take you through canal locks, where the tour guides demonstrate how the water can be raised and lowered.

The other parking option is the free lot across from the Old Angler's Inn, but that requires a two-mile hike along the C&O Canal towpath to the falls. This lot fills up by late morning with fishers, hikers and kayakers, so get there early. But beware, there is minimal shade on the path, so if it's a hot day, bring a hat, sunscreen and plenty of water.

One of my favorite hikes begins at Old Angler's Inn. Take the C&O Canal towpath in and then the Billy Goat Trail back out. Alternatively, you can begin at the visitor center.

# GREAT FALLS OVERLOOK

The overlook is a one-mile round trip from the Great Falls Tavern parking lot. The entire stretch is wheelchair accessible. The first half follows the C&O Canal towpath, taking you past four locks along the canal (Lock 20 is at the parking lot, and the turnoff for the overlook is at Lock 17). You then turn onto the boardwalk to the overlook. There is bicycle parking.

The boardwalk carries you over Falls and Olmsted Islands, serving to protect the delicate ecosystems. Periodic flooding carries away the trees, so smaller species such as shrub oaks tend to thrive here, as do prairie grass and some wetlands.

The view of the falls from the overlook is stupendous. The river churns and foams as it plunges past giant boulders and then races through narrow Mather Gorge below. Immediately opposite are the three Virginia overlooks, where a crowd has usually gathered. Look for kayakers in Mather Gorge below the falls.

# C&O Canal Towpath

From the Old Angler's Inn parking lot, begin the hike along the C&O Canal towpath. The path is flat and easy, and it is two miles from the inn to Great Falls Tavern. You'll pass the Widewater, the Potomac's channel before the last ice age. The C&O engineers opted to use this channel rather than dig a new one in the cliff for the canal. The Widewater is now a mile-long, four-hundred-foot-wide lake. The canal is placid, and expect to see turtles and waterfowl.

C&O engineers built six locks within one mile to bypass Great Falls. You will pass by these en route to the tavern, starting at Lock 15 and ending at Lock 20. This gives the section its name, "Six Locks."

Shortly after Lock 16, you will come to the "stoplock." This was a point in the canal where floodwaters could be diverted into the river. The pedestrian bridge marking the end of the Berma Road is overhead, and the northern end of the Billy Goat Trail starts here. Particularly fascinating is the giant stone aqueduct on which you are now standing. The river carved a sheer face out of the side of the mountain, so engineers built a seventy-foot buttressed wall to carry the canal across the cliff.

Continue past all six locks to the Great Falls Tavern Visitor Center at Lock 20, the Washington Aqueduct Dam and the falls overlook. Retrace your steps to the Angler's Inn. Or, if you're up for a challenge, take the turnoff to the Billy Goat Trail.

## *Billy Goat Trail: Section A*

Great Falls has three Billy Goat Trails. The best known—and the most difficult—is the one closest to the waterfall. This traverses Bear Island, which is co-owned by the Nature Conservancy and the National Park Service.

The rocky Billy Goat Trail is a strenuous, 1.7-mile hike that takes you along the cliffs above Mather Gorge and then plunges down steep hillsides to the riverbank below. There are many pull-off sites where the view of the Potomac beckons—and where rock climbers scale the heights in half a dozen places on the Virginia side. Note how smooth the rocks are; the river polished them over the millennia. This also makes them slippery and dangerous. Kids love this trail. Keep in mind to wear appropriate footgear! This means hiking boots. The trail is covered with rocks, and you will scale a cliff at one point. Bring plenty of water.

The Billy Goat Trail is a loop that connects with the C&O Canal towpath at its north and sound ends. You can begin at either end, but I suggest starting from the north, near the stoplock and pedestrian bridge. This is because of the steep, seventy-five-foot Spitzbergen Cliff that you will scale halfway along the hike. It's easier to scale going up than down. No special climbing gear is needed.

## Berma Road

The Berma Road, an old conduit road for the canal, begins at the Angler's Inn parking lot and runs parallel and slightly uphill of the C&O Canal for 1.5 miles until it reaches the pedestrian bridge near the stoplock. There the road joins the towpath. If you are on a bicycle, the Berma Road is the preferred route. It is flat and shaded and bypasses the rocks in the towpath near Lock 15. The view is good of the canal and the Widewater below.

## Gold Mine Loop

While the C&O towpath is almost always crowded, the Gold Mine Loop is just the opposite. The path is well marked and not strenuous. It winds through second-growth forest, where white-tailed deer abound and small streams cut ravines. The trail passes many interesting sites, including Civil War trenches and rifle pits, old roads and the defunct Maryland Gold Mine. As a bonus, the forested trail is entirely in the shade, making it much cooler in the summer than the exposed towpath. It is about a five-mile round trip, starting at the Angler's Inn.

A Union soldier camping near Angler's Inn discovered gold during the Civil War. He purchased the land in 1867. Eventually, about thirty mines removed some five thousand ounces of gold. The Maryland Gold Mine was opened in 1900 and closed in 1939. The remnants of this mine include several corrugated iron buildings and a water tower. The mine is also accessible by car. It lies directly opposite the intersection of MacArthur Boulevard and Falls Road.

## Billy Goat Trail: Section B

The least-traveled of the three Billy Goat sections, this 1.6-mile trail offers intimate views of the Potomac. It is mostly easy, flat and shaded, but there are many small rocks jutting from the trail. Wear proper shoes (no sandals).

The trail starts near the Angler's Inn parking lot and then loops down to the river before meeting back with the C&O towpath near the Marsden Tract campground. The entire loop is about 3.0 miles.

*How to get there: Great Falls is on MacArthur Boulevard, three miles west of Interstate 495 near the American Legion Bridge.*

## Carderock Recreation Area

The cliffs at Carderock are some of the oldest rocks along the Potomac basin. They began forming 450 million years ago as underwater volcanic sediment. As Africa and North America collided, the Mid-Atlantic region was pushed up, forming the Appalachian Mountains and the Piedmont.

Carderock is well known as a rock climber's paradise. There are a series of twenty-five- to forty-foot-high cliffs in the recreation area: Jungle Cliff, Hades Heights and Outlook Rock. On any given day, you can watch dozens of climbers scale the cliffs and rappel back down. This is a very good place to learn basic rock climbing skills under professional instruction.

## Billy Goat Trail: Section C

Carderock's hiking path is the third Billy Goat Trail, Section C. The Carderock trail is easy—just a three-mile round trip. It is fairly flat but has some rocks along the way, so wear appropriate shoes and bring water and snacks. The trail is mostly in the shade.

The hike begins above the rock climbing cliffs known as Jungle Cliff and Hades Heights and then heads south for 1.6 miles. The river is forty feet below and very placid; you are looking at a narrow branch and woodsy Vaso Island. Continue past the noisy shoals in the river until the path returns to the towpath of the C&O Canal. Turn left and follow the towpath back to the parking lot.

A worthwhile quarter-mile detour through nearly half a billion years of geology is located right by the western trailhead. When the Billy Goat Trail comes to a fork, the left takes you above the cliffs for the main trail. But if you take the branch to the right, it will curve around the base of Jungle Cliff and Hades Heights, where you'll see any number of rock climbers. Take a close look at the rocks, their sedimentary layers showing that this was once the bottom of the ocean, while the presence of quartz indicates that they were later under high pressure underground from a mountain chain that later eroded. Since the last ice age, the Potomac has carved into the rocks and smoothed their faces. Continue for a short distance until the trail dead-ends and then return the way you came.

*How to get there: Take the Clara Barton Parkway from I-495 toward Great Falls and then exit at the Carderock Naval Surface Warfare Center.*

# The Clara Barton Parkway

The Clara Barton Parkway is a nearly eight-mile-long roadway in Maryland that starts near Carderock and ends at Chain Bridge. After that, the road continues as Canal Road into Georgetown. Completed in 1989, it is actually part of the GW Parkway. It is named after Clara Barton, the president of the American Red Cross and one of history's great humanitarians; she lived along what is now the parkway.

## Seven Locks

For those who want to explore the C&O Canal without being overwhelmed by crowds, Seven Locks is an ideal destination. It is easy to reach, located on Clara Barton Parkway just below the American Legion Bridge. Park at either Lock 10 or Lock 8—or come by bike from Georgetown or Great Falls.

Seven Locks (Locks 8–14) dropped C&O canalboats fifty-six feet in just 1.25 miles. Assuming that you start at Lock 8, the round-trip walk or bicycle trip will be 2.50 miles along the shaded towpath. This is a very easy hike, as it is completely flat. Several lockhouses along the way housed families who operated the locks.

The Potomac Conservancy runs the River Center at Lock 8 in the historic 1830 lockhouse, which is open during summer months. This is an education center demonstrating the ecology of the Potomac. A few hundred feet downriver is Minnie's Island, an 8.5-acre island deeded to the Potomac Conservancy in 1994. "Everyone who owned it before us was in the CIA or the Senate," quipped Deanna Tricarico, who runs the River Center. A boat is required to visit the island, though in the winter months the river level drops, so you may be able to walk directly to the island.

At Lock 10, you can take a short detour to the river. This begins directly opposite the bridge next to the lockhouse and takes you to a peaceful inlet. Swainson's Island lies across the water. Lockhouse 10 is part of the Canal Quarters program, which allows overnight guests and is run by the C&O Canal Trust, the official nonprofit of the national park. It was remodeled in 1930s style from the Civilian Conservation Corps era. Other lockhouses in the program include 6, 22, 25, 28 and 49.

Note that a number of these locks, notably Locks 8 and 11, are red sandstone; they came from the same Seneca quarry that provided the stone for the Smithsonian Castle. There are also locks made from granite yet have red sandstone caps. Lock 11 has a lockhouse, along with an original mile marker for Mile 9, erected about 1830.

Locks 9, 10 and 12 are unique. These use "drop locks." A winch allowed a single person to operate the drop lock, which fell straight backward into the water, opening the lock for the canalboat to enter. Most locks on the C&O Canal are "swing locks," which required two people to open the gates using balancing beams, like a set of double doors.

An idyllic view of the C&O Canal near Washington. *Library of Congress.*

Lock 13 is directly below the American Legion Bridge, and the bridge supports straddle the lock to protect the canal. Lock 14 immediately follows. From there you can turn around and return to the parking area via the towpath. The more ambitious can continue on to Carderock; if you combined Seven Locks with the Billy Goat Trail Section C, you'd hike about five miles round trip.

*How to get there: Seven Locks and the River Center is at 7906 Riverside Drive in Cabin John, Maryland, directly off the Clara Barton Parkway. Park at Lock 8 or Lock 10.*

# CABIN JOHN BRIDGE

Cabin John Bridge carries MacArthur Boulevard over the Cabin John Creek in a single lane. It is part of the ten-mile Washington Aqueduct that brings water from Great Falls to Dalecarlia Reservoir. Built from 1857 to 1864, it has a single 220-foot-wide span and is one of the most beautiful bridges in the area. The parapet consists of Seneca red sandstone, while the granite arch was imported from Massachusetts. As the aqueduct was completed during the Civil War, it was long known as the Union Arch.

*How to get there: Take the Clara Barton Parkway west from Chain Bridge; Cabin John Bridge is shortly after the Clara Barton National Historic Site. You can also drive over it on MacArthur Boulevard.*

Washington Aqueduct built the graceful Union Arch, better known as the Cabin John Bridge, to carry drinking water to Washington, D.C. *Library of Congress.*

# CLARA BARTON NATIONAL HISTORIC SITE AND GLEN ECHO PARK

Often overlooked by many Washingtonians are two unique sites in one: Clara Barton National Historic Site and Glen Echo Park. Separated only by a parking lot, these sites have a common history through the Chautauqua movement. This late nineteenth-century program brought speakers and classes to numerous sites around the country, building on the Methodist camp meeting. The Glen Echo facility opened in 1891, and its stone tower still remains.

Clara Barton was a remarkable woman, the "Angel of the Battlefield" who brought nursing supplies to countless wounded soldiers during the Civil War. She was a workaholic.

A portrait taken in 1904 of Clara Barton, former president of the American Red Cross and one of the world's greatest humanitarians. *Library of Congress.*

Barton once wrote, "You have never known me without work; while able, you never will." She lobbied Congress to ratify the Geneva Convention and establish the American Red Cross. She served as the organization's president from 1881 to 1904, providing relief during eighteen disasters and the Spanish-American War. Barton retired at the age of eighty-two.

Drawn by the Chautauqua movement, Barton established a large house adjacent to Glen Echo in 1891 to serve as a warehouse and headquarters for the American Red Cross. She lived at the house for the last fifteen years of her life (1897–1912), and the house is open daily for tours. Barton should be counted among America's greatest citizens and was certainly one of the world's great humanitarians.

Across the parking lot is Glen Echo, the only amusement park preserved as a national park. It operated from 1898 to 1968 and saw many architectural additions over the years, though the park today is preserved as it was in the 1940s—thus the numerous art deco buildings.

Glen Echo is best remembered for its role in the civil rights movement. Privately owned, the park denied entrance to African Americans. In 1960,

Clara Barton built a warehouse for the American Red Cross in Glen Echo that then became her home. *Library of Congress.*

Howard University students and civil rights advocates led a mass sit-in at the Dentzel Carousel. This led to five weeks of protests that led to full integration at the park a year later. Bring your camera; Glen Echo is fascinating to photograph. It also offers a wide range of classes and performing arts.

*How to get there: Take the Clara Barton Parkway west from Chain Bridge and then exit at MacArthur Boulevard and follow the signs.*

## LOCK 6 AND LITTLE FALLS

Great Falls is far better known than its downstream cousin, Little Falls, yet both provided major obstacles to commerce on the Potomac. The river narrows significantly in the Potomac Gorge, and the waters drop swiftly through Little Falls.

George Washington's Potowmack Company, organized in 1785 to improve navigation on the river, decided to do something about the problem. The first improvement built was the Little Falls Skirting Canal. This 2.5-mile-long canal was the longest in the Potowmack Company system and had three locks. It was completed in 1795. This was later incorporated into the C&O Canal, starting at Lock 5.

On July 4, 1828, President John Quincy Adams ceremoniously broke ground for the C&O Canal near what is now Lock 6. On the same day, the Baltimore and Ohio Railroad was inaugurated in Baltimore. This was not a coincidence. Baltimore feared that the C&O would divert trade to Georgetown. The race was on for the Ohio River—one that the B&O would win, reaching Cumberland in 1842, eight years before the C&O. This was a major gamble for Maryland: railroads were a new technology, and they were untested. Canals, on the other hand, had been used in Europe and the United States since the 1760s.

Lock 6 and its adjacent lockhouse mark the true beginnings of the C&O, and they operated until 1924. Today, Lockhouse 6 has been meticulously restored as part of the Canal Quarters program that hosts overnight guests. Adjacent to the lockhouse is Lock 6 Trail, a short path that parallels the feeder canal and Dam No. 1 that fed the C&O and powered much of Georgetown's industry. The feeder canal is a popular kayaking slalom course.

A quarter mile upriver from Lock 6 is the Little Falls Dam, built by the U.S. Army Corps of Engineers in 1959 as part of the Washington Aqueduct. It creates a pool of water that is then pumped to Dalecarlia Reservoir for treatment. In 2000, a twenty-four-foot notch was cut for migrating fish. The dam is a mile upriver from Little Falls.

*How to get there: Lock 6 is on the Clara Barton Parkway, one mile west of Chain Bridge.*

# Chain Bridge

One of the first bridges to link both sides of the Potomac was built directly below Little Falls in 1797. It was a natural site for a bridge—one of the narrowest points across the river, as the fall line squeezes the river into a swiftly moving channel barely ninety feet wide. Floodwaters destroyed the bridge and its successor, so a new type of bridge was built. Stone towers were erected in the river, and wrought-iron chains suspended the bridge below, thus earning the nickname "Chain Bridge." This structure only lasted two

Union soldiers guard the Chain Bridge over the Potomac, then built of railroad ties. *Library of Congress.*

years before another flood carried it away, as well as two others of similar design. Before the Civil War, a heavy timber bridge made from railroad trusses was constructed, the sixth bridge. In total, there have been eight bridges built at the site. The latest—and longest lasting—was built in 1939.

Pimmit Run spills down the palisades on the Virginia side of Chain Bridge. Thomas Lee purchased a land grant here in 1719 that later featured a tobacco warehouse and the first industrial site in Arlington. The Declaration of Independence and other key federal papers were hidden there overnight while the British burned Washington on August 24, 1812. A short but rock-strewn walk on the Potomac Heritage Trail leads to an overlook of the site's ruins.

*How to get there: From Washington, D.C., take Canal Road, NW, and watch for the signs. From Arlington, Virginia, take Glebe Road or the GW Parkway north to the bridge.*

# THE GW PARKWAY

Better known as the GW Parkway, the George Washington Memorial Parkway is administered by the National Park Service. It is a divided roadway that starts at Great Falls and ends at Mount Vernon, George Washington's plantation and home. It parallels both sides of the Potomac and features many historic sites and scenic views along the route.

In 1930, Congress authorized the purchase of the Potomac shore in Virginia from Great Falls to Mount Vernon. It did this to provide public recreation and to prevent development along the scenic river shore. The original sixteen miles of the parkway opened in 1932 from Arlington Memorial Bridge to Mount Vernon. It used the latest highway construction methods (including divided lanes, two on each side) and was hailed as "America's Most Modern Highway."

In the 1950s, the highway was extended northward to Interstate 495 (the Capitol Beltway), and it is now twenty-five miles long in Virginia. The GW Parkway was then expanded into Maryland; the eight-mile-long Clara Barton Parkway was completed in 1989. Today, the GW Parkway encompasses 7,600 acres of protected parkland.

*Author's note: I've arranged this chapter in an unusual order, but there is a method. Many sites along the GW Parkway face the river, and you can only access many of them from the northbound lanes of the parkway. Thus I've split the chapter into two segments: northbound from Roosevelt Island to Turkey Run Park and southbound from the Iwo Jim Memorial to Mount Vernon.*

# GW PARKWAY: FROM ROOSEVELT ISLAND TO TURKEY RUN

## *Theodore Roosevelt Island*

Directly across the Kennedy Center for the Performing Arts is Theodore Roosevelt Island. It is a ninety-one-acre tranquil preserve surrounded by a bustling and noisy city, with cars crossing the Roosevelt Bridge and planes flying into National Airport. It is the largest island in the Potomac and has two miles of hiking trails.

The local Indians named the island Analostan and fished the river there. The Mason family bought the island in 1717 and operated a ferry service to Georgetown. John Mason, the fourth son of George Mason and president of the Potowmack Company, inherited "Mason's Island" in 1792. He built a large brick manor house as his summer home, garden and working plantation, while his main residence was in Georgetown. Mason built a causeway connecting the island to Virginia, but stagnant water and precarious finances drove the Masons off the island in 1832. The causeway was removed in the 1970s.

Union soldiers stand on a rock on Mason's Island (now Roosevelt Island), facing Georgetown across the Potomac. *Library of Congress.*

During the Civil War, the Union stationed United States Colored Troops on the island, fearing that Washingtonians would be disturbed at the sight of armed black soldiers. The Mason manor burned down during the war. "Contraband" (escaped slaves) were also quartered on the island.

In 1932, the Theodore Roosevelt Memorial Association bought Mason's Island as a memorial to the former president and conservationist. He did much to preserve the natural beauty of the United States and set aside 234 million acres as national parks and public lands.

Today, the island is covered in dense second-growth forest. There is a monument to Roosevelt in the center of the island. From there, head south on the Woods Trail leading to just under the Roosevelt Bridge and then swing north on the Swamp Trail, an elevated path through the wetlands. You'll have excellent views of the Kennedy Center. Finally, complete the loop across the northern part of the island with views of Georgetown and the Key Bridge.

*How to get there: Theodore Roosevelt Island is directly off the northbound GW Parkway. There is also a pedestrian bridge from Rosslyn.*

## Potomac Overlook Regional Park

Potomac Overlook Regional Park may be small, but it is rich in history. An Indian camp was excavated in the 1960s, and arrowheads and pottery were found. Indians made this a summer camp from about 500 BCE to 500 CE. Sitting on a bluff above the Potomac, the site offered farmland, fresh water and flood protection and was close to the superb fishing grounds at Little Falls.

There are several trails, none of which is long or strenuous, that begin at the Nature Center. A short Heritage Loop passes the Indian Spring and ends at the Indian camp. Another path winds past the Donaldson Cemetery (used 1877–1962) and then to the Potomac Overlook.

The best path takes you down the Donaldson Run Trail, past a dismantled concrete dam and under the GW Parkway until you reach the Potomac Heritage Trail, which parallels the river shore. The Potomac here is swift and narrow; you may see dozens of people fishing along the banks, as it is a popular fishing hole. This trail is about a one-mile round trip. Or continue downriver along the Potomac Heritage Trail half a mile until you see large rusted metal boilers, used to power steam drills in a nearby quarry until 1938.

*How to get there: Potomac Overlook Regional Park is at 2845 Marcey Road in Arlington, Virginia.*

## Fort Marcy

Fort Marcy is one of the sixty-eight forts built around the District of Columbia during the Civil War. On September 24, 1861, Union troops began building the fort, which is the northernmost fort on the Virginia side. It protected the strategically vital Chain Bridge. An artillery battery of seventeen guns and three mortars was stationed here. The fort never came under Confederate attack.

During the Civil War era, Fort Marcy overlooked farmland; today it is a thick forest, blocking any view of the Potomac. The earthworks have been preserved, though they have eroded in places. The interior is now a grassy area with picnic tables and several brass cannons. A rifle trench still exists north and west of the fort. The blue-blazed Potomac Heritage Trail runs past along the GW Parkway.

There are a number of other Civil War forts in the ring surrounding the nation's capital. They include Fort Ward in Alexandria, Fort Foote in

The Union built a ring of sixty-eight forts around Washington during the Civil War. Artillerists man a cannon at Fort Carson. *Library of Congress.*

Maryland and Forts Dupont and Stevens in Washington. The latter was the only fort to come under attack.

Beyond Fort Marcy, there are several other sites to see along the northbound GW Parkway. The Potomac Heritage National Scenic Trail parallels the parkway 8.5 miles between Roosevelt Island and the American Legion Bridge. It connects to a network of trails leading all the way to Algonkian Regional Park. Claude Moore Colonial Farm is a tobacco demonstration farm from the eighteenth century. Finally, Turkey Run Park has the headquarters for the GW Parkway, as well as several trails through the thick woods along the river.

*How to get there: Fort Marcy is accessed from the northbound GW Parkway four miles past Rosslyn. There is no southbound entrance.*

# GW Parkway: From Iwo Jima to Mount Vernon

The GW Parkway south of Roosevelt Island has most of the sites along the roadway. It can be explored by car but ideally on the Mount Vernon Trail by bicycle.

## *U.S. Marine Corps War Memorial & Netherlands Carillon*

Just north of Arlington National Cemetery—and immediately adjacent to the Theodore Roosevelt Bridge and GW Parkway—is the Iwo Jima Memorial. Dedicated in 1954, it is a large bronze statue of the marines planting the American flag atop Mount Suribachi on February 23, 1945. The marines present a sunset concert and review parade on the grounds during summer evenings.

Nearby is the Netherlands Carillon, a steel bell tower dedicated by the people of the Netherlands in 1960 for the United States' role in World War II. It has a stunning view of the District and Arlington National Cemetery and a straight shot of the Lincoln Memorial, Washington Monument and Capitol. The carillon is open two hours each day in summer, when a carillonneur plays the bells. The bell tower is only accessible via a long staircase. The grassy slope leading down to the Potomac is also an ideal place to watch the Fourth of July fireworks, unless you are lucky enough to watch from a boat in the river.

## Arlington House: The Robert E. Lee Memorial

In 1802, George Washington Parke Custis—the step-grandson of George Washington—began building a classical, Roman-style mansion on a 1,100-acre plantation that his father, John Parke Custis, had purchased in 1778. Arlington House sits on a hill with an excellent view of the Potomac and Washington beyond. Custis named it Arlington House after the family property on the Eastern Shore and completed the Greek Revival building in 1817. The house gives Arlington County its name (before 1920, it was Alexandria County).

Custis's daughter, Mary Anna Randolph Custis, married Robert E. Lee in the family parlor in 1831. The couple lived there the next thirty years, and six of their seven children were born in the house. When the Civil War broke out in 1861, Lee took command of Virginia's military forces and left the house, never to see it again. The occupying Union army made Arlington House the headquarters for the defenses of Washington and confiscated the property in 1864. Two hundred acres were set aside as a military cemetery. Arlington National Cemetery was born.

Lee's eldest son, George Washington Custis Lee, sued the federal government in 1882 over the confiscation of his family's property. His suit was successful, but rather than retain the property inside a national cemetery, Lee accepted a $150,000 settlement. The National Park Service began administering the house in 1933.

The 624-acre cemetery on the hillsides surrounding Arlington House contains the graves of hundreds of thousands of U.S. politicians, sailors and soldiers. At the base of Arlington House are the graves of John F. Kennedy, Robert and Jackie. Nearby is the grave of Pierre L'Enfant, the man who designed Washington, D.C. He was exhumed and reburied there in 1909. Arlington Memorial Bridge connects Arlington National Cemetery to the Lincoln Memorial. Built in 1932, it is the most beautiful bridge on the Potomac.

## Mount Vernon Trail

The Mount Vernon Trail is an 18.5-mile paved trail that begins at Key Bridge and ends at Mount Vernon, parallel to the GW Parkway. It is entirely in Virginia. Expect to see cyclists, runners and walkers sharing the crowded trail. South of Alexandria, however, the crowds thin. The Mount Vernon Trail provides an alternative to driving the GW Parkway and, in fact, is a vastly different experience. The trail is on the riverside, providing magnificent views, and there are many places to stop along the way.

Paralleling the GW Parkway was the Alexandria Canal, which operated from 1843 to 1886 to connect the C&O Canal in Georgetown to the port of Alexandria.

## Columbia Island

Columbia Island is a narrow island that begins near the Iwo Jima Memorial and ends at the Humpback Bridge on the GW Parkway. It is entirely parkland. On the eastern side is the Potomac, while the Boundary Channel is to the west. Arlington Memorial Bridge crosses over the island, and the Mount Vernon Trail passes underneath it.

Farther south is Lady Bird Johnson Park. The former first lady selected the site for the Lyndon Baines Johnson Memorial Grove. The park has a good view of Washington's skyline and is popular for picnickers and sun tanners.

Adjacent to the Humpback Bridge on the GW Parkway is the Navy and Marine Memorial. This beautiful statue of seagulls flying over waves was added in 1934 to commemorate the thousands of American sailors who have lost their lives at sea.

Opposite the Columbia Island Marina lies the Pentagon. The United States won World War II from this massive five-sided building, the largest office building in the world, completed in 1943 after just seventeen months of construction. Reinforced concrete was made from sand dredged from the Potomac. Tens of thousand of people work in the 6.5-million-square-foot building that covers twenty-nine acres—surrounded by sixty-seven acres of parking lots. It sits just downriver from Arlington National Cemetery on land that housed an African American community (Queen City), wetlands, a dump, a USDA experimental farm and Washington Hoover Airport. It was also one of the sites attacked on 9/11.

## National Airport

After Columbia Island, the Mount Vernon Trail passes under the Fourteenth Street Bridge, formerly the Long Bridge. At its base was once a seedy part of Arlington called Jackson City, where gambling, prostitution and saloons were rampant. Near this spot, Air Florida Flight 90 crashed into the Potomac after striking the bridge on a snowy January 13, 1982, killing seventy-eight people. The trail bends to the right around Gravelly Point. The point is just north of National Airport and is a good place to watch airplanes take off and land. But it is noisy! On one side is the Potomac, on the other is Roaches Run Waterfowl Sanctuary.

Ronald Reagan Washington National Airport opened in 1941 on 450 acres of landfill deposits in the Potomac. The art deco main terminal is a monument to the era. The Mount Vernon Trail passes by the airport; two footbridges afford great views of the airport and of Washington beyond. The inland part of the airport was once Abingdon plantation, and there are historic markers near the parking garages. The house stood there for 190 years but burned down in 1930. George Washington's stepson, John Custis, owned Abingdon, and Custis's daughter, Nelly, was born there.

## The Road to Alexandria

Just south of National Airport is the inappropriately named Four Mile Run (it is really nine miles long). This urban stream is polluted from silt and runoff from suburbia. Arlington County's sewage treatment plant is located near the end of the creek. The last several miles of the run is an ugly sunken concrete channel built by the U.S. Army Corps of Engineers in the 1970s to prevent the stream from overflowing its banks. A bike path follows Four Mile Run throughout Arlington; much of it is pleasant, as the stream parallels green parkland. Alexandria and Arlington are working to restore Four Mile Run to its natural setting.

Almost one mile beyond Four Mile Run is Daingerfield Island. Though technically no longer an island, the 107-acre preserve has ballparks, boating facilities and the Washington Sailing Marina. The Mount Vernon Trail is built on a platform over a marsh and then proceeds to Alexandria.

# ALEXANDRIA

Alexandria was established in 1749, and a seventeen-year-old George Washington helped survey the town. It rapidly grew into a premier river port. By the end of the eighteenth century, it was the country's seventh-largest port; its position helped entice the federal government to establish its new seat of administration directly across the Potomac. Alexandria's nickname is still Port City.

Old Town Alexandria retains its historic eighteenth-century architecture and street grid. It is especially lovely to walk the quieter city streets and admire the brick architecture. The streets are fairly steeped in history: George Washington kept a townhouse at 508 Cameron Street, and Robert E. Lee's boyhood home was at 607 Oronoco Street. President Thomas Jefferson celebrated his inaugural banquet at Gadsby's Tavern (138 North Royal Street) in 1801. Towering over Old Town is the George Washington Masonic National Memorial.

During the War of 1812, Royal Navy captain James Gordon sailed seven warships up the Potomac to assist with the raid on Washington. Alexandria was defenseless, and having seen how Washington was burned several days before, the city capitulated to Gordon on August 27, 1814. The British confiscated ships and immense supplies from Alexandria's warehouses during the five-day occupation of the city.

Alexandria rivaled Georgetown for trade, and the C&O Canal gave Georgetown an advantage. Alexandria raised the stakes by digging the Alexandria Canal, which linked Alexandria to the C&O Canal from 1843 to 1886. This terminated in the northern part of Old Town. An office complex, Alexandria Canal Center, includes the restored Tidal Basin and lock and is adjacent to Oronoco Bay Park.

Alexandria City and Alexandria County (now Arlington County) were appropriated into the new national capital in 1791. But as no federal buildings were constructed on the Virginia side, Alexandria wanted to return to Virginia—especially as Port City was a major slave-trading center. Congress retroceded the Virginia portion of the district to Virginia in 1846.

An overhead photo of the port of Alexandria in 1919. *Library of Congress.*

The Torpedo Factory Art Center in Alexandria, Virginia, was once part of a complex that manufactured torpedoes during World War II. *Garrett Peck.*

Though Alexandria's sympathies were with the South, Port City was crucial for Washington's safety. The day after Virginia's referendum to leave the Union on May 23, 1861, Union forces crossed the Potomac and occupied the city. Colonel Elmer Ellsworth tore down a Confederate flag from the Marshall House Hotel but was then confronted by the owner, James Jackson, who shot him dead. A private bayoneted Jackson. The death of these two men marked the first casualties of the Civil War. Union forces built a ring of sixty-eight forts around the capital. Fort Ward in Alexandria still survives as a park and museum, and it is the most intact of all the forts.

International shipping changed considerably after World War II, and Alexandria's small port facilities could no longer compete. No longer an active seaport except for the Robinson Terminal, Alexandria has preserved much of its extensive waterfront as parkland. Waterfront Park is at the base of Prince and King Streets. Built in 1919, the Torpedo Factory produced for World War II 9,920 torpedoes, which were tested at Piney Point downriver. It was converted into an art center in 1974 to help revitalize the waterfront. Just to the north are Founders Park and Oronoco Bay Park. Alexandria is developing a three-mile park along the city's shoreline, from Dangerfield Island to Jones Point Park.

*How to get there: Alexandria is six miles south of Washington, D.C., on the GW Parkway. If you visit Alexandria by bicycle, the Mount Vernon Trail takes you through Old Town along Washington Street. A better option is to veer off onto the River Route, which parallels the city's waterfront all the way to Jones Point.*

# Jones Point Park and
# the Woodrow Wilson Bridge

Jones Point Park is a sixty-acre tract just south of Old Town Alexandria off the GW Parkway. Many Native American tools have been excavated there, indicating that this was a preferred place for fishing and hunting. In 1682, Cadwalder Jones built a trading post at the point, which has since been named after him. Jones Point was used for shipbuilding from the 1700s until World War I. A lighthouse operated from 1836 to 1925 to warn ships of sandbars. The current lighthouse was built in 1856 and has been restored. According to the original plan for the District of Columbia, Jones Point was the southernmost point of the district. There is a plaque commemorating this and a boundary stone.

Overlooking the Potomac was Battery Rodgers, one of the Civil War–era forts erected to protect the nation's capital. Jones Point later had a 1,200-foot-long building used as a ropewalk to assemble hemp into rope. During World War I, the Virginia American Shipbuilding Corporation built ships at the point.

The Jones Point Lighthouse in Alexandria marked the southernmost point in Washington, D.C. *Library of Congress.*

The twin-spanned Woodrow Wilson Bridge towers over Jones Point. It was opened in 2006 and 2008, replacing its aging predecessor from 1961. The 1.1-mile-long bridge is one of two Potomac crossings on the Capitol Beltway—the other is the American Legion Bridge. There is a bike and pedestrian lane on the north side of the ridge with three pull-off areas to stop and take in the view, along with interpretive signs; this begins near the Freedman's Cemetery at the base of the bridge. Look for the bronze markers in the pavement noting the borders of D.C., Maryland and Virginia, which converge on the bridge.

*How to get there: The Woodrow Wilson Bridge is on the Capitol Beltway (I-495) south of Washington. Park at Oxon Hill Farm (Maryland) or Jones Point Park (Virginia) and walk or bike across.*

## Bell Haven and Dyke Marsh

Just south of Alexandria on the GW Parkway are Belle Haven Marina and Dyke Marsh. Belle Haven started in the 1730s as a tobacco warehouse; there was an earlier colonial fort from the 1600s nearby. A mooring basin was converted into the marina, which is today a place to rent boats and take sailing lessons. The view from the picnic area looks across a wide bay to Jones Point and the Woodrow Wilson Bridge. The bay is tidal, and there are almost always hundreds of birds feeding and swimming in the shallow water. This is an excellent place to bird watch.

Dyke Marsh Wildlife Preserve is a 380-acre wetland and nature preserve that Congress set aside in 1959. The marsh is fed from Hunting Creek, which empties into the Potomac to the north. But the marsh isn't completely natural—it was created after failed attempts to create farmland and a shad fishery. A farmer built an earthen dike around the lowland to grow crops on land claimed from the river. Eventually, the landowners gave up on maintaining the dikes, and much of the land eroded. A 650-acre marsh then developed (almost half of it was destroyed by dredging). Today, Dyke Marsh is the largest tidal freshwater marsh in the Washington area.

Almost three hundred species of birds make their home in the preserve, along with 260 varieties of plants. September is the peak month for bird watching. Thousands of birds stop along the Potomac during their annual fall migration. The birds are most active around sunrise and sunset.

About one-third of Dyke Marsh today is underwater except during low tide. The floodplain is occasionally inundated, and it is covered with cattails and wildflowers. Farther inland is a swamp forest of deciduous trees. The walking path through Dyke Marsh was formerly the Haul Road, used in the 1960s to dump debris into the marsh. It is an easy two-mile round trip. It begins at Belle Haven Marina and proceeds south through the forest before swinging east into the marsh. Every Sunday at 8:00 a.m., naturalists from Friends of Dyke Marsh lead walking tours.

*How to get there: Bell Haven Marina and Dyke Marsh are two miles south of Old Town Alexandria on the GW Parkway.*

# River Farm

River Farm was the northernmost of George Washington's five farms, a 1,800-acre plantation that he purchased in 1760 and immediately leased out. It lay directly astride the King's Highway that linked Georgia to New York. In 1919, Malcolm Matheson purchased the property, renovated the house (known as Wellington) and built the formal gardens. He decided to sell the property in 1971. The interested buyer? The Soviet Embassy. Congress and the State Department intervened, asking Matheson to reconsider. Two years later, the American Horticultural Society bought River Farm for its headquarters and showcase gardens.

River Farm is now a lovely twenty-five-acre Potomac park. On the property are two White House gates cast in 1819 that came to the farm in 1937. The gardens change with the seasons, and a walk down to the river passes through a meadow crowded with wildflowers. Down the street (8301 East Boulevard Drive) is the Collingwood Library and Museum on Americanism, also once part of River Farm.

*How to get there: River Farm is at 7931 East Boulevard Drive, just off the GW Parkway four miles south of Alexandria.*

# Fort Hunt Park

Fort Hunt is a 156-acre park with artillery batteries dating to the Spanish-American War of 1898. Directly across the Potomac in Maryland is the massive Fort Washington. The two forts were a choke point against any enemy ships advancing up the river. Fort Hunt was used during World War II as an interrogation point for captured Germans. Many of the interrogators were German Jews who had fled Nazi Germany in the 1930s. Today, much of the park is picnic and athletic facilities.

*How to get there: Fort Hunt Park is two miles north of Mount Vernon on the GW Parkway.*

# Washington and the Potomac

In 1791, Congress decided to establish a national capital midway between the North and South. It was a compromise of historic proportion: southerners allowed the federal government to assume state debts incurred from the American Revolution, and northerners agreed to put the new capital on the Potomac—at the geographic center of the country at the time, but also in the slaveholding South.

President George Washington selected the location for the District of Columbia, centered on Tidewater farmland between Georgetown and the Eastern Branch (Anacostia). This would become the city of Washington. He chose the site over Williamsport, Hagerstown and Sharpsburg, Maryland. It was also the closest location to his home at Mount Vernon.

Washington hired Pierre L'Enfant to lay out the plan for the city. L'Enfant was a French officer who fought for the United States during the War of Independence. He designed a city of grand avenues and monumental views—a grid interspersed with diagonal avenues and many circles and squares. He sited the Capitol and President's House on two high points and designed a canal through the city. At the city's center was a National Mall, a large public space that later became known as "America's Front Yard." Construction on the new capital began in 1792. L'Enfant feuded with the city commissioners and the underhanded schemes of Thomas Jefferson, and he was removed eleven months into the job. But his impression on the city was permanent.

The district was originally one hundred square miles, a perfect square measuring ten miles on each side. Two-thirds of the land was in

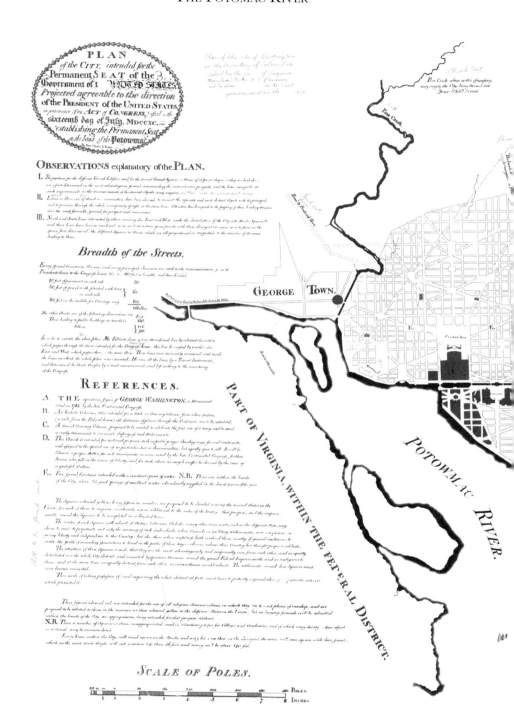

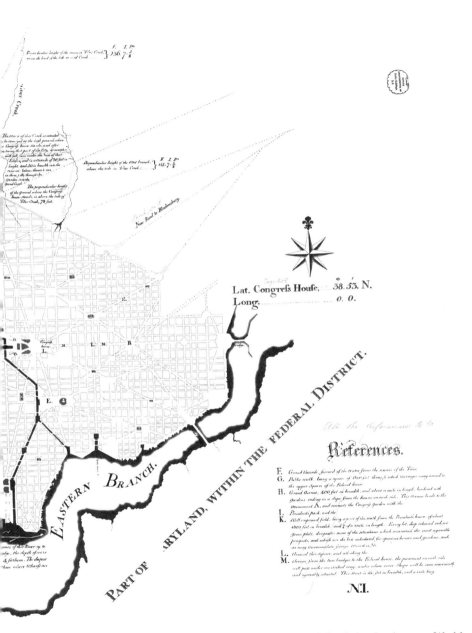

Pierre L'Enfant designed the federal city that became Washington, D.C. *Library of Congress.*

Maryland, while the rest was in Virginia. In 1846, the federal government returned the Virginia portion, Alexandria County (now Arlington County) and Alexandria city. The public buildings were largely built by African slaves.

Andrew Ellicott surveyed the new city in 1791 and 1792, assisted by the African American astronomer Benjamin Banneker. Ellicott laid forty boundary stones, placed at one-mile intervals. Many of the stones are still in place today; since 1916, the Daughters of the American Revolution have erected fences to protect them. The stone is sandstone from the Public Quarry on Aquia Creek, a quarry that L'Enfant acquired for the city's public buildings. John Adams became the first president to serve in the new capital. He and Congress moved there in 1800, the year after George Washington's death.

# GEORGETOWN

Georgetown was founded in 1751, forty years before Washington, D.C. Its most notable landmarks are the towers of Georgetown University, established in 1787, the same year as the U.S. Constitution.

Although it is best known today for its shopping and nightlife, Georgetown was once a harbor and industrial town. It had numerous flour mills, a rendering plant, a soap factory, a cotton mill, a paper mill and limekilns. There are many remnants of Georgetown's industrial past; look no further than the pleasant walk along the C&O Canal towpath, just a block away from bustling M Street. You can see the many factories and warehouses that were converted into office buildings and apartments.

Henry Foxall built a foundry in 1801 (C&O Mile 1.5) to supply cannons for the military. When the British raided Washington in August 1814, a thunderstorm flooded Rock Creek, saving his foundry from destruction. He sold the foundry the next year to John Mason, a son of George Mason. When the C&O Canal was built right through his property, Mason was superbly situated to receive pig iron from the Antietam Iron Works.

Georgetown was the farthest ships could navigate up the Potomac, and thus it made sense for the C&O Canal to terminate there. Georgetown's four canal locks were all made with sandstone from the Public Quarry on Aquia Creek. The oldest bridge in the city, built in 1831, carries Wisconsin Avenue over the C&O Canal. The major good hauled on the canal was coal, which largely went to heat Washington in winter and

*Above*: A close-up of one of Fort Frederick's four bastions. Built in 1756 during the French and Indian War, the fort was never attacked. *Garrett Peck.*

*Below*: The view from the Netherlands Carillon looks over the Potomac, the Lincoln Memorial, the Washington Monument and the Capitol. *Garrett Peck.*

*Above*: The Potomac begins at this tiny trickle in the Alleghenies, marked by the Fairfax Stone. *Garrett Peck.*

*Below*: The Interstate 68 road cut through Sideling Hill reveals millions of years of sedimentary layers. *Garrett Peck.*

*Above*: One of George Washington's favorite views was from Prospect Peak overlooking the Potomac, three miles from Berkeley Springs. *Garrett Peck.*

*Below*: Williamsport, Maryland, was a major port along the C&O Canal, and at its center was the Cushwa warehouse at the loading and turning basin. *Garrett Peck.*

*Above*: An overhead view of Antietam National Battlefield, showing the Sunken Road, or Bloody Lane. *Garrett Peck.*

*Below*: John Brown was captured at the U.S. Arsenal's engine house at the end of his raid on Harpers Ferry. *Garrett Peck.*

*Above*: The most beautiful structure on the C&O Canal is the seven-arched Monocacy Aqueduct. *Garrett Peck.*

*Below*: Hundreds of ferries once carried traffic across the Potomac; today, only White's Ferry still operates. *Garrett Peck.*

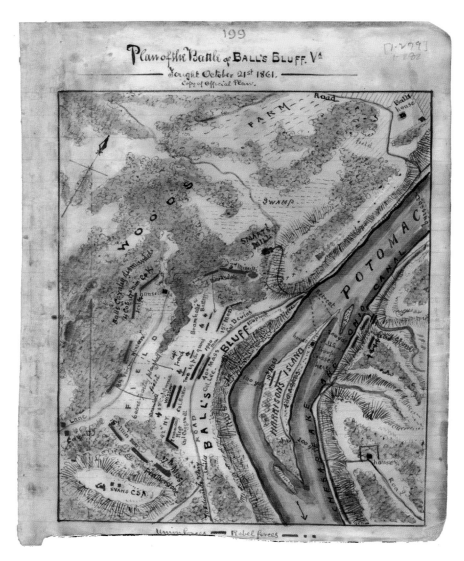

A color map showing the Union and Confederate positions during the Civil War Battle of Ball's Bluff. *Library of Congress.*

*Above, left*: The red ruins of the Seneca stone cutting mill at the Seneca quarry. Stone for the Cabin John Bridge and the Smithsonian was cut here. *Garrett Peck*.

*Above, right*: Made from Seneca red sandstone, the Seneca Aqueduct is the only aqueduct on the C&O Canal that is also a lock. *Garrett Peck*.

*Left*: The very recognizable bright-red Smithsonian Castle building in Washington, D.C., made from Seneca red sandstone. *Garrett Peck*.

*Above*: Great Falls is the most dramatic feature on the Potomac. *Garrett Peck.*

*Below*: A close-up of a kayaker traversing the Fish Ladder at Great Falls during the Potomac Whitewater Festival. *Garrett Peck.*

*Left*: A rock climber scales an ancient cliff at Carderock. *Garrett Peck.*

*Below*: Glen Echo Park is the only amusement park in the national park system and was the site of a key civil rights protest in 1960. *Garrett Peck.*

*Above*: Built next to the Car Barn in Georgetown, these stairs were made famous in the horror movie *The Exorcist*. *Garrett Peck*.

*Opposite, top*: Ice in the Potomac as seen from Key Bridge near Georgetown during the week of President Barack Obama's inauguration. *Garrett Peck*.

*Opposite, middle*: The C&O Canal ends at the Tide Lock at Rock Creek. Beyond it is the Watergate complex and the Kennedy Center. *Garrett Peck*.

*Opposite, bottom*: Built in 1932, the Memorial Bridge is the most beautiful bridge on the Potomac, connecting the Lincoln Memorial to Arlington National Cemetery. On the hill in the distance is Arlington House. *Garrett Peck*.

*Above*: Abolitionist Frederick Douglass purchased this Anacostia house, Cedar Hill, in 1877 and lived there until his death in 1895. *Garrett Peck*.

*Below*: The oldest tombstone in Congressional Cemetery marks the grave of William Swinton, who died in 1807. The sandstone tombstone came from the Public Quarry in Aquia. *Garrett Peck*.

*Above*: Boardwalks lead to Kingman and Heritage Islands in the Anacostia River, created from dredged soil in 1916. *Garrett Peck*.

*Below*: A cherry tree in full bloom near the Capitol Columns at the National Arboretum. *Garrett Peck*.

*Above*: A Piscataway sweat lodge marks the site of the Accokeek Creek Site, the most significant Indian archaeological find on the Potomac. *Garrett Peck*.

*Below*: Bethlehem Steel built a salvage basin to recover iron from the Mallows Bay ship graveyard. *Garrett Peck*.

*Left*: Built in 1836, the Piney Point Lighthouse is the most endearing lighthouse on the Potomac. *Garrett Peck.*

*Below*: The lighthouse at Point Lookout marks the mouth of the Potomac. *Garrett Peck.*

*Above*: George Washington's home, Mount Vernon, is the most recognizable building on the Potomac. *John DeFerrari.*

*Below*: George Mason built Gunston Hall on Mason Neck and wrote the Virginia Declaration of Rights, which became the model for the Declaration of Independence. *Garrett Peck.*

Built in 1831, the C&O Canal's bridge carrying Wisconsin Avenue over the canal is the oldest surviving bridge in Washington, D.C. *Library of Congress.*

Two C&O Canal locks in Georgetown in 1925, a year after the canal closed for good. *Library of Congress.*

power Georgetown's industries. The National Park Service now operates a small visitor center and offers canal rides from April to October. Nearby is a small bust of Supreme Court justice William Douglas, who helped save the canal in 1954.

During the C&O Canal's heyday in the 1870s, Georgetown became a choke point as canalboats lined up, sometimes for days, to pass through the final four locks. In 1876, an inclined plane was built west of Georgetown to lower canalboats directly into the Potomac. It operated until the flood of 1889. There is a historic marker near Mile 2 on the canal towpath.

Abolitionists, including Methodists and Quakers, helped slaves escape to freedom along the Underground Railroad. In Georgetown, Mount Zion United Methodist Church (1334 Twenty-ninth Street, NW) was an African American church founded in 1816 and a stop along the Underground Railroad. Oak Hill Cemetery nearby has a burial vault where escaped slaves hid.

Francis Scott Key, the composer of "The Star-Spangled Banner," lived in Georgetown. The Key Bridge connecting Georgetown to Rosslyn, built in 1923, is named for him, as is a small park. His house was torn down in 1947. Across the street from the bridge is the Car Barn, a building that housed trolleys when Washington had an extensive streetcar system. Adjacent to the building are the stairs made famous by the movie *The Exorcist*.

Directly upriver from Key Bridge are the remains of the Alexandria Canal Aqueduct, which moved canalboats seven miles downriver from Georgetown to Alexandria. It operated from 1843 to 1886 and after that was converted for vehicle use. The aqueduct was torn down in 1933, as the Key Bridge made the viaduct no longer necessary. Just a few stone pilings are left in the river, as well as a remnant in Georgetown.

In 2000, the National Park Service acquired Georgetown Waterfront Park, a mile-long former harbor and industrial zone. The park is now a pleasant river walk and urban park. The Whitehurst Freeway towers over the park. In the 1950s, an interstate highway was to have crossed the Potomac at a newly built Three Sisters Bridge and then connect with the Whitehurst. That, fortunately, did not happen. It would have changed the look of the river and Georgetown permanently.

There are three places to rent canoes and kayaks near Georgetown: Thompson Boat Center and Jack's Boats, both in Georgetown proper, and Fletcher's Boat House just beyond C&O Mile 3 (this is reputedly one of the best fishing holes in the Potomac). You can row from Key Bridge to the Three Sisters, three large stone clusters in the river, and then down

Two gentlemen meet on a muddy trail in Rosslyn in the 1860s, overlooking the Alexandria Aqueduct and Georgetown. *Library of Congress.*

around Roosevelt Island and back—or down to National Airport for a lengthier excursion. Next to the Thompson Boat Center at the mouth of Rock Creek is the Tide Lock on the C&O Canal. This is where the C&O Canal begins (and ends).

For bicyclists, the paved Capital Crescent Trail parallels the C&O towpath from Key Bridge to the Maryland border and then swings up to Silver Spring. This eleven-mile path was formerly the Georgetown Branch of the Baltimore and Ohio Railroad.

# Rock Creek and Foggy Bottom

Georgetown's eastern border is Rock Creek, once known as Piney Creek. Beyond that is Foggy Bottom, a neighborhood name that always gets a laugh from visiting tourists but whose origin was as marshy lowland where the fog hovered. The marsh has long been filled in.

Foggy Bottom started as the village of Hamburgh. It has steadily evolved over two centuries, from dock facilities to industry to government, university and international institutions. The Washington Branch of the C&O Canal once cut along the neighborhood's waterfront, but that was closed in 1870 and filled in to form Constitution Avenue. Foggy Bottom was then largely taken over by industry—Washington Gas Works and two breweries were among the neighborhood's biggest employers. Though a small historic district preserves some of the working-class brick houses, much of Foggy Bottom has been taken over by large institutions.

Rock Creek National Park is now a major commuter route, though there is a wide paved trail paralleling the road, popular for cycling and running. There were once many mills along the stream, as the land around it was farmed until the 1930s.

Just beyond Rock Creek is the Watergate complex and the Kennedy Center. In 1965, construction began on the Watergate on the former site of the Washington Gas Works. The Watergate is best known for the 1972 break-in to the Democratic National Committee offices. The investigation by *Washington Post* journalists Bob Woodward and Carl Bernstein, fueled in part by the secret source nicknamed "Deep Throat" (interim FBI director Mark Felt), led to Nixon resigning in 1974 rather than face impeachment. Felt and Woodward often met in the middle of the night in a Rosslyn parking garage (1401 Wilson Boulevard in Arlington).

The site of the John F. Kennedy Center for the Performing Arts was once the city's largest brewery, the Christian Heurich Brewing Company, which operated there from 1895 to 1956. The brewery was demolished in 1961 for the new performing arts center. The Kennedy Center has a terrace roof; you can walk all the way around it and see magnificent views of the district and Virginia.

# The National Mall

Pierre L'Enfant's plan for the district included a National Mall along the Potomac shoreline. His design changed significantly over the following centuries, and subsequent grand plans for the Mall were never built. The result is a mishmash of monuments, museums and vast, vacant public space. "We add things here and there—but no one says, 'How do we hold it together?'" says Judy Feldman, president of the National Coalition to Save Our Mall.

The Potomac was much wider than it is now: the Washington Monument was right on the shoreline, and the White House was close to the river at the mouth of Tiber Creek. Near the White House—extending from Constitution Avenue to the World War II Memorial into what was the Potomac—was the Seventeenth Street Wharf, built in 1806–7. Workers building the Washington Monument found many Indian artifacts, indicating that the site was once a popular Indian fishing hole.

L'Enfant envisioned a grand monument to George Washington as an oasis at the Mall's center, one with trees and landscaped grounds. The monument was built from 1848 to 1884 in two major phases; you can visibly see where the stone changed. Construction was halted during the Civil War with only one-third of the monument complete. It is the world's tallest obelisk at 555 feet high and is the dominant architectural feature in the city. Sadly, the landscaping and oasis were never built, and you approach the monument from a vast, unwelcoming and unshaded plane. Near the Washington Monument is the Smithsonian Castle, built in 1847 from Seneca red sandstone.

L'Enfant also envisioned a canal to carry riverboat traffic through the city from Georgetown to the Anacostia waterfront. The Washington Canal was opened in 1815, a year after the British burned the capital during the War of 1812. It started at the Potomac just below the White House at Tiber Creek and then headed east along what is now Constitution Avenue. Near the Capitol, it turned southeast down to the Navy Yard. Starting in 1833, the Washington Branch connected the Washington Canal to the C&O through Foggy Bottom. The canal gradually silted up by the 1870s, and it became an open sewer that drained much of Washington's waste. The canal was filled in and is now Constitution Avenue. The only remnant is the lockkeeper's house at Seventeenth Street and Constitution.

Just behind the lockkeeper's house is a levee begun in 2011 to protect Washington against a catastrophic flood. This includes a stoplock that can be closed—this is one of the lowest points in the city, and the levee serves as a cork to keep a flooding Potomac from pouring in.

Once the Potomac Gorge ends around Georgetown, the river widens into a tidal estuary. At low tide, it had large mud flats and malaria-filled swamps. In an era that saw wetlands as a menace to public health,

The McMillan Plan of 1901 envisioned an expanded National Mall and a monumental core. *Library of Congress.*

Congress funded a massive reclamation project that began in 1882. Sand and silt from the Potomac were dredged to fill in the wetlands west of the shoreline. The landfill narrowed the river's width by half. The Washington Monument, once on the shore, was now half a mile inland. A crescent-shaped island was created out of mud flats. Engineers shaped the Tidal Basin within the new shoreline.

The reclamation project created a great deal of land, and for more than a decade, Congress debated what to do with it. Pierre L'Enfant had created a National Mall that extended from the Capitol to the Potomac shore, but in his day that was Seventeenth Street. Senator James McMillan led a commission to decide how to use the new land. The result was the McMillan Plan of 1901.

The McMillan Plan expanded the Mall to the west and south, creating two new parks: West Potomac and East Potomac Parks. Eventually, memorials to significant Americans were built atop this landfill, including the Lincoln Memorial overlooking the Potomac and the Jefferson Memorial on the Tidal Basin. Today, the Mall measures more than seven hundred acres and is known as "America's Front Yard," but we still haven't executed a comprehensive plan for the Mall more than two centuries after L'Enfant designed the federal city.

The Mall is geographically close to the Potomac but unfortunately has little to do with it. The Mall intersects the river nearly perpendicularly at the Lincoln Memorial; another access point is at the Jefferson Memorial, and below that at East Potomac Park. The Tidal Basin, while one of the loveliest spots in the district, looks inward on itself rather than out to the river.

It is difficult for pedestrians to get around the Mall: the closest Metro (subway) station is at the Smithsonian, and people then have to walk great distances to reach the memorials, with little relief or shade. Many people choose to drive instead. Commuter routes like Rock Creek Parkway and Ohio Drive take up much of the Potomac shore and make it dangerous for cyclists and pedestrians to reach the river. The monumental staircase leading from the river up to the Lincoln Memorial as a grand "watergate" is difficult to reach and rarely used.

From the 1930s to 1965, summertime concerts were played on the watergate barge near the Memorial Bridge, a floating concert hall with an acoustic shell. The audience sat on the staircase. Concerts came to an end because jet planes began flying into National Airport. Jet engines are deafening, so federal authorities ordered them to fly directly over the Potomac for the noise reduction. The concert barge was towed away.

"The Mall was a polyglot place, a series of leisure zones offering meandering walks amid well-tended groves and gardens fringed by working

A crowd gathers on the steps of the Lincoln Memorial to hear a concert played on the Watergate concert barge. *Library of Congress.*

operations such as railroad stations, greenhouses, arboretums, and even brothels," wrote Kirk Savage in *Monument Wars*. These were cleared away by the 1930s and replaced with grand views and grass. During World War II, the Mall was crowded with ugly temporary office buildings for defense workers. These, fortunately, were torn down afterward.

Today, the Mall is crowded with museums and monuments to people, presidents and wars. The big three are secular temples to presidents: a blank Egyptian obelisk for George Washington, a Greek temple for Abraham Lincoln (1922) and a Roman temple for Thomas Jefferson (1943). The latter two have larger-than-life statues, as if they were gods. The Lincoln Memorial was especially important during the civil rights movement. Marian Anderson's Easter concert in 1939 was held there, and Martin Luther King Jr. gave his "I Have a Dream" speech that capped the 1963 March on Washington.

Every sort of monument is found in this increasingly crowded field. The Vietnam Veterans Memorial (1982) is a large gash, like an open wound in the earth, but it is also therapeutic. The World War II Memorial (2004) is abstract and victorious. The realist Korean War Memorial (1995) shows a squad of wary infantrymen marching through a rainy landscape. The FDR Memorial (1997) is a seven-acre maze and rock garden. The MLK Memorial (2011) is purely allegorical: King emerges on the Stone of Hope from the Stone of Despair.

The "monumental core," as Kirk Savage called it, emerged in the decades after the McMillan Plan, with the Washington Monument at its center. The Capitol and Lincoln Memorial are at either ends of the longer east–west axis, while the White House and Jefferson Memorial are on the shorter north–south axis. The museums of the Smithsonian Institution define the borders. The Mall is vast and grand, but nothing about it feels natural: the elm trees are lined up in formal rows, and the ground is covered in rectangular cuts of grass. There is little shade for pedestrians to take shelter from the oppressive summer heat. Hundreds of thousands of visitors to the Smithsonian Folklife Festival and Fourth of July fireworks leave the grass heavily trampled and dusty.

There certainly is beauty along the Mall, even if it is man-made. The Tidal Basin offers one of the most pleasant walks in the nation's capital. The mayor of Tokyo gave three thousand Japanese cherry trees to the city in 1912, and this attracts millions of tourists every April for the Cherry Blossom Festival. Numerous memorials sit on the basin's periphery, including those dedicated to Thomas Jefferson, George Mason, Franklin

Delano Roosevelt and Martin Luther King Jr. (again, remember that all of this is landfill). There was once a whites-only beach along the Potomac during the Jim Crow era, but rather than comply with a Congressional law requiring it to allow blacks to use it, the city closed the beach.

## WATERFRONT

The city's historic waterfront in Southwest was on the Potomac and Anacostia Rivers, east of the Long Bridge (now the Fourteenth Street Bridge). The British burned the bridge during their raid on Washington on August 24–25, 1814, during the War of 1812, but it was soon rebuilt. As commercial shipping on the Potomac faded, there was no longer need for major harbor facilities in Washington. The waterfront now largely supports pleasure vessels.

Docked at the Gangplank Marina is the former presidential yacht USS *Sequoia*, now in private hands and rented for chartered excursions. It was built in 1925 and has served every president since Herbert Hoover. At the southern end of the waterfront is the Titanic Memorial, dedicated in 1931 and moved from near the Kennedy Center in 1966.

Across Washington Channel is East Potomac Park, an island created from dredging in the 1880s. The park is popular for recreation; you'll see many cyclists and runners, as well as golfers and swimmers. The island's southern tip is Hains Point, named for Peter Hains, the U.S. Army Corps of Engineers officer who oversaw the Potomac dredging.

### *Fort Lesley J. McNair*

Just south of the waterfront and west of the Navy Yard was the arsenal at Greenleaf (Buzzard) Point, established in 1791. British forces occupied Washington during the War of 1812 and sought to destroy the arsenal, but a tremendous explosion killed about thirty British soldiers. Another explosion killed twenty-two women there on June 17, 1864. A year later, the conspirators who assassinated President Abraham Lincoln were imprisoned, convicted and hanged at the arsenal. The arsenal was closed in 1881, and there are few historic buildings left. Fort Lesley J. McNair now occupies most of Buzzard Point and faces Washington Channel.

# Anacostia

## *The Forgotten River*

The Anacostia is often called the "forgotten river." Long neglected and once clogged with sewage, silt and toxic waste, the river has seen a comeback in its health since the late twentieth century. Originally known as the Eastern Branch, the Anacostia River is a broad, tidal tributary to the Potomac, an urban river that meanders past power plants and development, and yet much of its shoreline is preserved as parkland. It originates at Sandy Spring in northern Montgomery County, and 82 percent of the Anacostia watershed is in Maryland. The Northeastern and Northwestern Branches join at Bladensburg to form the Anacostia. The river then runs 8.5 miles to reach the Potomac.

A small Indian tribe, the Nacotchtanks, lived along the river when John Smith explored the region in 1608. He found the Anacostia teeming with life and remarkably clear and deep, its banks dense with trees.

As the nation's capital was being built, the U.S. Navy realized that the Anacostia was an excellent deep-water harbor and so built the Washington Navy Yard on its banks. Land along the river was once used for small farms and plantations. Development came much later, in part because the region was geographically isolated from the rest of Washington. That changed as bridges were built over the river at Benning Road and Pennsylvania Avenue. The third bridge over the Anacostia, the Navy Yard (Eleventh Street) Bridge, opened in 1818. As the new nation's capital grew, the Anacostia rapidly silted in, so much that ships could no longer make it to Bladensburg.

One of the major landowners in the Anacostia region was William Marbury, whose holdings included Blue Plains. President John Adams made him a midnight appointment as justice of the peace, but the incoming administration of Thomas Jefferson refused to recognize the appointment. Marbury sued, and in 1803, the U.S. Supreme Court issued its most important decision, *Marbury v. Madison*, establishing judicial review. (Marbury lost the case.)

The federal government purchased land in 1852 to build a hospital for the mentally ill: St. Elizabeths, on Congress Heights. This is today a closed facility that also houses the Department of Homeland Security.

In 1854, a local developer named John van Hook began the city's first Anacostia suburb. He built a small, whites-only community named Uniontown that connected to Washington via the Navy Yard Bridge. Many homebuyers worked at the yard. Most of the region was still agricultural. In 1886, Uniontown was renamed Anacostia.

During the Civil War, the Union built a chain of sixty-eight forts to protect Washington, including thirteen forts along the ridge east of the Anacostia River. Thousands of "contraband" (escaped slaves) made their way to Washington. Many of them settled along the river. After the war, General Oliver O. Howard, head of the Freedmen's Bureau, bought land on Barry's Farm to settle freed slaves just west of historic Anacostia.

During the Great Depression, World War I veterans descended on Washington to demand bonuses. The Bonus Army camped on the Anacostia Flats east of the river (now Anacostia Park). In July 1932, the U.S. Army cleared the campsite with tanks and tear gas.

The Anacostia region remained largely rural through the 1940s. In the 1950s, as urban renewal displaced the working-class black population in Southwest Washington, many of the people were resettled east of the Anacostia. The area is mostly African American today.

Once-toxic sites such as the Navy Yard have been cleaned up. The main problem with the Anacostia today is that raw sewage enters the river after thunderstorms—a product of the city's original sewage system from the 1870s. Garbage flows out of the storm drains, bringing with it industrial contaminants as well. The Anacostia Watershed Society (AWS) has been working since 1989 to clean up the river, carting away tons of debris every year and lobbying for environmental change. D.C. Water is building the Clean Rivers Project, a massive underground system to divert sewage from overflowing into streams. The river is slowly improving, but silt from suburban storm runoff is still a major problem.

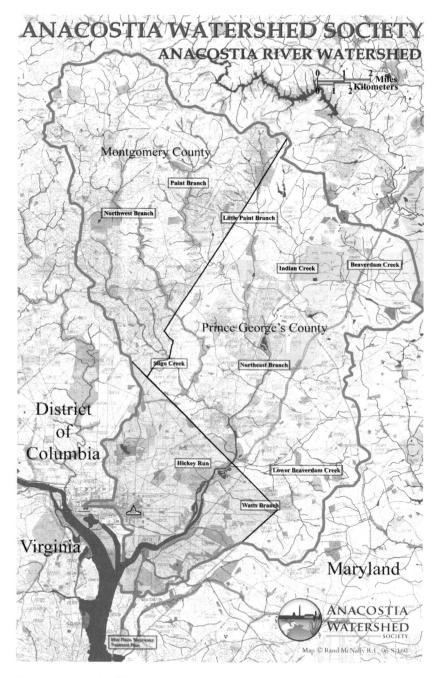

Long known as the "forgotten river," the Anacostia is recovering from decades of pollution, sewage and silt. Most of its watershed is in Maryland. *Anacostia Watershed Society.*

Washington is making efforts to clean up the river and improve the riverfront, drawing people to a natural gem of the city, in part by creating the Anacostia Waterfront Corporation in 2004. Two stadiums are on the Anacostia: RFK and Nationals Ballpark. The latter in particular is helping fuel redevelopment of the long-neglected Anacostia waterfront. Rowing and yacht clubs line the banks, and fishermen are returning. The core is the Anacostia River Trail, a twenty-mile trail along both sides of the river. You can begin this by bicycle at the Navy Yard.

# WASHINGTON NAVY YARD

Founded in 1800, the Washington Navy Yard is the oldest naval facility in the United States. For its first twenty-nine years, its commandant was Thomas Tingey, a naval officer born in Great Britain who had served in the Royal Navy before immigrating to the United States. He commanded a squadron of ships in the Caribbean to protect American shipping during the Quasi-War with France. This earned him a promotion to build a shipyard in the new nation's capital along the Anacostia.

Tingey built the Navy Yard from scratch. He oversaw construction and outfitting of the budding nation's navy. The facility's architect was Benjamin Latrobe, the same man leading construction of the Capitol. The Navy Yard became one of the largest employers in the city. A few blocks north were built the Marine Barracks at Eighth and I Streets to protect the yard and man the ships. Henry Foxall's cannon foundry in Georgetown supplied heavy guns.

As British soldiers entered Washington on August 24, 1814, during the War of 1812, Tingey set fire to the Navy Yard to keep the ships and supplies from being captured. He quickly rebuilt the yards, and shipbuilding resumed. He died in 1829 and is buried at Congressional Cemetery.

The Navy Yard (Eleventh Street) Bridge connected to the eastern shore of the Anacostia, where many workers had their homes. John Wilkes Booth fled over the bridge after assassinating Abraham Lincoln.

Shipbuilding at the Navy Yard had all but ceased by the time of the Civil War, and the facility was used for making boilers and guns and outfitting ships. It was also one of the most heavily polluted industrial sites in the district, and the Environmental Protection Agency declared it a Superfund Site. A cleanup project began in the 1990s to remove contaminants.

There has been a construction boom around the Navy Yard since the late 1990s, when Congress began appropriating money to refurbish the facility and add office space. Inside the Navy Yard is the National Museum of the U.S. Navy and the original Latrobe-designed buildings. The Anacostia River Trail passes along the waterfront, where you'll find the museum ship USS *Barry*. Just to the west of the Navy Yard is Nationals Park, which opened in 2008. Diamond Teague Park and Yards Park, a modern urban park with a fascinating pedestrian bridge, draw the waterfront into a continuous park.

*How to get there: Washington Navy Yard is located on M Street, SE, near the Navy Yard Metro station.*

# FREDERICK DOUGLASS NATIONAL HISTORIC SITE

Abolitionist Frederick Douglass was known as the "Sage of Anacostia" after he moved to Washington in 1877. *Library of Congress.*

Known as Cedar Point, this Victorian home was built in about 1859 on a prominent Historic Anacostia hilltop overlooking Washington with a tremendous view of the city. After a long career supporting the abolitionist cause, Frederick Douglass was appointed the U.S. marshal for the District of Columbia in 1877. He purchased Cedar Point and lived there until his death in 1895. The National Park Service now administers the house.

Douglass was probably the most important African American of the nineteenth century. He was born into slavery in about 1818 and taught himself to read. He escaped from Baltimore with the help of Anna Murray, his future wife, and went on to a distinguished career publishing and speaking about the evils of slavery. Douglass's sons, Charles and Lewis, served in the Fifty-fourth Massachusetts (the black regiment depicted in the movie *Glory*) during the Civil War.

Douglass was known as the "Sage of Anacostia" and the "Lion of Anacostia" for his silvery mane. He controversially married a white woman, Helen Pitts, in 1884. It was Helen who helped preserve the house and Douglass's legacy after his death. The house today is open for tours and filled with many belongings from Douglass's life. Behind the house is the Growlery, a stone hut where Douglass retreated to write.

Nearby is Fort Stanton Park, one of the sixty-eight Civil War forts that ringed the nation's capital. The Anacostia forts are connected by a hiker-biker trail. The most significant surviving fort in the Anacostia chain is Fort Dupont, which has four hundred acres of parkland and extensive earthworks.

*How to get there: The Frederick Douglass House is at 1411 W Street, SE, in Washington, D.C.*

# CONGRESSIONAL CEMETERY

Truly a gem on the eastern side of Capitol Hill, Congressional Cemetery has been in active use for more than two centuries—and more than fifty-five thousand people are buried there, from statesmen to ordinary citizens. The first tombstone, for William Swinton in 1807, is believed to be sandstone cut from the Public Quarry on Government Island at Aquia.

A who's who of Washingtonians is interred at the cemetery—more than seven hundred Civil War veterans, pre-prohibition brewers, prostitutes and victims of the Spanish flu epidemic. Lincoln assassination accomplice David Herold is buried there. Prominent Washingtonians like Navy Yard commandant Thomas Tingey, photographer Matthew Brady, Marine Band leader John Philip Sousa and FBI director J. Edgar Hoover and his partner, Clyde Tolson, have their last resting spots in the cemetery. Nearby is a corner for gay veterans, including Leonard Matlovich, who died in 1988; his famous epitaph reads, "When I was in the military they gave me a medal for killing two men and a discharge for loving one." Frank Kameny, the gay civil rights leader, is also interred there.

There are also dozens of cenotaphs, or empty tombs, designed by Benjamin Latrobe and made of Aquia Creek sandstone to remember congressmen and senators who died in Washington. Congressional Cemetery is fun and quirky, and frankly it is more enjoyable than Arlington National Cemetery, whose overwhelming scale is uniformly solemn. The cenotaphs, tombstones and vaults are intriguingly different, many of them works of art. Local historian Ruth Ann Overbeck's granite obelisk is near the entrance; she listed no date, only this command: "Look it up!" Guided tours are held on Saturdays, although the park is open daily for self-guided tours.

*How to get there: Congressional Cemetery is at 1801 E Street, SE, in Washington, D.C.*

# KINGMAN AND HERITAGE ISLANDS PARK

Created in 1916 from soil that the U.S. Army Corps of Engineers dredged from the Anacostia River, Heritage and Kingman Islands are tranquil nature preserves surrounded by wetlands. During World War II, local inhabitants grew "Victory Gardens" on the islands. The northern half of Kingman Island includes Langston Golf Course—the oldest public golf course in the country. A short footbridge crosses to Heritage Island and then another to Kingman Island. There are trails to explore both. Heritage Island has a 0.5-mile loop trail; Kingman has a 0.7-mile (one-way) trail.

*How to get there: From downtown Washington, take East Capitol to RFK Stadium and then park in Lot 6. The entrance is along the river. Alternatively, come by bicycle on the Anacostia River Trail.*

# U.S. NATIONAL ARBORETUM

The U.S. National Arboretum is a 444-acre sanctuary run by the U.S. Department of Agriculture. The U.S. Army Corps of Engineers began developing the arboretum in 1927, although it was only opened to the public in 1959. It is a great place to see the cherry blossoms in early April if the crowds at the Tidal Basin are too much. The park overlooks the Anacostia River. The arboretum is spectacular in all seasons; in spring there is always something in bloom, while in fall the deciduous forests turn vibrant colors. There are numerous hiking paths, and it is also pleasant to explore by bicycle.

The arboretum has specially planted collections around the site. These include Asian, azaleas, boxwoods, conifers, dogwoods, hollies, magnolias, native plants and perennial collections. There is also a friendship garden, the National Herb Garden, the National Bonsai and Penjing Museum and the National Grove of State Trees. Several sites offer views over the Anacostia River.

The centerpiece is the Capitol Columns that stand atop a grassy hill like a Greek temple. These twenty-two columns came from the east portico of the U.S. Capitol, which was expanded in 1958. The columns were removed to storage and then brought to the arboretum in 1984.

*How to get there: The National Arboretum is at 3501 New York Avenue, NE, in Washington, D.C.; there is another entrance off Bladensburg Road on R Street, NE.*

# KENILWORTH AQUATIC GARDENS

Kenilworth Aquatic Gardens is the only national park for cultivated aquatic plants. The park covers seventy acres and has more than forty-five ponds that are filled with waterlilies and water lotuses. It resides on the east bank of the Anacostia, directly opposite the National Arboretum.

The gardens began in the late 1800s when a one-armed Civil War veteran, Walter Shaw, planted waterlilies in an abandoned ice pond. He added more ponds and soon had a thriving business with his daughter, Lucy Helen Fowler. When the U.S. Army Corps of Engineers sought to seize the gardens and dredge the Anacostia in the 1930s, Helen lobbied Congress to intervene. In 1938, Congress purchased the gardens for $15,000 and renamed it Kenilworth.

The waterlilies bloom in May, but the park gets especially popular in mid-July at the peak of the lotus bloom. Crowds of photographers capture images of these amazing blossoms. They are best photographed in the morning. The park has two short walks. One goes through the ponds filled with lotuses and lilies and leads to a boardwalk through Kenilworth Marsh. The other is a 0.7-mile River Trail (one-way) that skirts around the marsh, ending with a view of the Anacostia.

*How to get there: Kenilworth Aquatic Gardens is at 1550 Anacostia Avenue, NE, in Washington, D.C.*

# BLADENSBURG

The Historic Bladensburg Waterfront sits directly on the Anacostia, a remnant of a thriving harbor. Bladensburg was once a deep-water port and slave-trading center founded in 1742, older than either Alexandria or Georgetown. The town is just below the juncture of the Northwest and Northeast Branches, marking the beginning of the Anacostia.

Wealthy merchant, rope maker and shipbuilder Christopher Lowndes built the mansion Bostwick on a hill overlooking the port in 1746. The first secretary of the navy, Benjamin Stoddert, later owned the house. Bostwick is still there (3901 Forty-eighth Street), though behind the railroad tracks, so it has lost its view. The Anacostia Watershed Society has its headquarters right on the river in the George Washington House (4302 Baltimore Avenue), built in 1732.

Opposite Bladensburg is the town of Colmar Manor. A stream known as Dueling Creek flows through the town—Washington's elite settled their differences just outside the nation's capital (dueling was illegal in the district). More than two dozen duels were held there. The most famous was between navy commodores James Barron and Stephen Decatur on March 22, 1820, in which the latter was fatally wounded.

The Anacostia was once forty feet deep at Bladensburg, but tobacco farming silted up the river, ending Bladensburg's days as a port by the mid-nineteenth century. A major flood struck the town in 1953, and the U.S. Army Corps of Engineers built high levees in response. Suburban development in Montgomery and Prince George's Counties sends a great deal of silt down the river. Through this flows the Anacostia in a narrow, shallow channel, surrounded by broad fields of muck. "We can't blame agriculture anymore," said Brent Bolin of the Anacostia Watershed Society. "This is suburbanization that you're looking at."

## The Battle of Bladensburg

To avenge the American burning of York, Canada, during the War of 1812, British Royal Navy admiral Alexander Cochrane sailed up the Chesapeake Bay with a large fleet to attack Washington. He discharged a small army of 4,500 men at Benedict on the Patuxent River under General Robert Ross and Admiral George Cockburn, who marched overland to attack the nation's capital from the east. The Americans burned the Benning Road and Pennsylvania Avenue bridges over the Anacostia but somehow left the Bladensburg bridge intact.

General William Winder commanded the American army, mostly inexperienced militia, and hastily deployed on ground overlooking Bladensburg to the west (now Colmar Manor) as the British stormed the bridge on August 24, 1814. President James Madison followed to watch the fight. The militia was quickly routed, the only serious resistance coming from Commodore Joshua Barney and five hundred seamen who had burned their barges two days earlier on the Patuxent. The battle became known as the "Bladensburg Races" for the speed at which the Americans fled. The British marched into the capital and burned the public buildings and then marched out the next night to rendezvous with the fleet.

*How to get there: Bladensburg Waterfront Park is at 4601 Annapolis Road in Bladensburg, Maryland. The Anacostia River Trail connects to the park.*

## *Canoeing the Anacostia*

The Anacostia Watershed Society leads canoe tours on the Anacostia, including the John Smith Voyage and Kingfisher Trails. Kingfisher is a five-mile paddle that begins at Bladensburg and ends at Anacostia Riverfront Park. It takes you past the Kenilworth Aquatic Gardens, the National Arboretum, the massive PEPCO plant and Kingman and Heritage Islands. Other trips begin from the Anacostia Community Boathouse, just below Congressional Cemetery.

The Anacostia is lined on both sides with stonework from the U.S. Army Corps of Engineers. The river is only several feet deep but has so much silt that you can't see the bottom. What may surprise you is how much wildlife exists along the waterway: bald eagles, blue herons, cormorants, ducks, geese, kingfishers and ospreys. There is hope for the Anacostia.

# Plantations on the Potomac

Tobacco plantations dominated the colonial economy in the coastal plain below Little Falls. Production was very labor-intensive, so a large number of African slaves worked the fields. Tobacco farming depleted the soil and silted up the streams, and the quality of the leaf had dropped by the late eighteenth century. Some plantation owners like George Washington shifted to wheat and other crops.

The Potomac served as a watery commercial artery for plantations. The houses always faced the river and often had a dock. Many ships plied the river, picking up crops and delivering manufactured goods. The river served as a gateway to market and the world. Farmers attempted to make their plantations self-sufficient. Never entirely successful, they relied on imported luxury goods such as spices, tea, coffee, furniture and silks, most of which were imported from Great Britain or the West Indies.

A number of plantation homes still survive along the Potomac shore in Virginia. These include Mount Vernon, Gunston Hall, Rippon Lodge and Woodlawn. All but Woodlawn were designed by Richard Blackburn. William Fairfax's mansion, Belvoir, no longer exists, though it now lends its name to Fort Belvoir.

## Mount Vernon

Along with the White House and Thomas Jefferson's Monticello, Mount Vernon is the best-known presidential home in America. George

Washington's half brother, Lawrence, built it. After Lawrence died in 1754, George inherited the property and took possession of it in 1761 after Lawrence's widow, Ann Fairfax, died. He called it his home until his death there in December 1799. Washington also had significant absences from the plantation during the French and Indian War, while leading the Continental army during the War of Independence (1775–83) and during his two terms as president (1789–97). Mount Vernon was a working plantation with hundreds of slaves.

In many ways, the United States was fortunate with Washington. He understood the limitations of power; though some wanted him to be a king, he recognized that this would simply replace King George III, and that wasn't why he had fought and ultimately won the War of Independence. His role was crucial at the 1787 Constitutional Convention in Philadelphia that created our federal system of government that divides power among three branches, each with checks and balances against the others. Once elected as the nation's first president, he stepped down after two terms, handing the office to John Adams in a peaceful transfer of power.

We think of Washington as an old man from the portraits of him and the one-dollar bill, but as a young man, he was full of ambition to make a name for himself. At sixteen, he began surveying for the Fairfax family, and a year later he helped lay out the city of Alexandria. He commanded Virginia's forces in the French and Indian War (1755) at the age of twenty-three. In fact, his actions instigated the war when he attacked a French contingent near Fort Duquesne (Pittsburgh)—later he was forced to surrender at Fort Necessity.

As an ambitious young man from a second-tier colonial aristocratic family, Washington aimed high when he proposed marriage to the wealthy twenty-seven-year-old widow Martha Dandridge Parke Custis. She was formerly married to the richest planter in Virginia, Daniel Parke Custis, and had two children with him, Martha Dandridge Custis and John Park Custis. George and Martha married in 1759. He became stepfather to her two children but never had children of his own. She also brought a large number of dower slaves and much property. Washington ambitiously expanded Mount Vernon from a simple farmhouse into a mansion suitable for colonial gentry. He did this somewhat on the cheap: Mount Vernon is a wooden building, not brick or stone.

Washington saw the Potomac as the key to opening the West. After the Revolution, he took a trip in September 1784 to inspect and collect rents from his vast properties. When he returned to Mount Vernon, his head was filled with ideas for linking the Potomac to the Ohio River. He addressed the Virginia legislature, requesting that the commonwealth approve the charter of a Potowmack Company. Maryland supported the plan as well, and in March 1785, commissioners from both states met at Mount Vernon to outline the terms of trade along the Potomac. They subsequently reached the Mount Vernon Compact.

The compact became one of the key legal arguments for Virginia's use of the Potomac River. Though the Potomac is entirely within Maryland, that state agreed that Virginia could use the river as long as it did not obstruct navigation. This was designed to promote trade, but its impact is lasting even to today, as both states draw water from the river. The Mount Vernon Compact provides the legal framework.

As president of the Potowmack Company, Washington pushed through the development of the Little Falls Skirting Canal on the Maryland side and the Great Falls Skirting Canal on the Virginia side, as well as additional navigation improvements farther up the Potomac River at Seneca Falls, Shenandoah Falls and House Falls. Roads were terrible, rutted, muddy things. The way to travel was by river.

Washington died in 1799. His will freed the slaves he directly owned—fewer than half of the 316 who toiled at Mount Vernon—on January 1, 1801. The rest were owned by the estate of his wife's first husband or were on loan from other plantations. He tried to send a message to other slaveholders that they should free their slaves as well, but few followed his lead. When Martha died, some slave families were separated when they were divided among Washington's four grandchildren.

Today, the mansion and two hundred acres are all that is left of Washington's once vast eight-thousand-acre plantation along the Potomac. The estate gradually declined; the buildings were in sad shape and badly in need of restoration. In 1853, a mother and daughter—Louisa and Ann Pamela Cunningham—founded the Mount Vernon Ladies' Association to save the mansion from neglect. The association acquired Mount Vernon in 1860 for $200,000.

Mount Vernon is said to have launched the movement for historical preservation, as this was the first time in the nation's history that a national treasure was preserved for the public. The Mount Vernon Ladies' Association still administers the home and grounds.

Tours of the house are brief—docents whisk you from room to room—but the great pleasure of seeing Mount Vernon is exploring the grounds and the Museum and Education Center. There are numerous walking trails around the property, including those to the upper and lower gardens, George and Martha's tomb, the slave memorial and burial ground, the forest trail and the wharf. The view across the bowling green is perhaps the best known at Mount Vernon. There is also a magnificent view of the river from the mansion itself.

*How to get there: Mount Vernon is eight miles south of Alexandria, at the end of the GW Parkway and the Mount Vernon Trail.*

## George Washington Grist Mill State Park

As tobacco declined, George Washington turned to growing wheat to keep his Mount Vernon plantation profitable. He built a gristmill on Dogue Creek to export flour. In 1797, Washington's plantation manager, a Scot named James Anderson, suggested that he distill whiskey next to the gristmill. Washington agreed; the first small batch sold so well that Washington ordered a larger distillery built in October 1797. The following year, he produced four thousand gallons of rye whiskey and, in 1799, almost tripled that to eleven thousand gallons. It was enormously profitable: this last batch earned $7,500. This made Washington the whiskey king of the Potomac. The distillery burned down in 1814 but was rebuilt and dedicated in 2007.

*How to get there: George Washington Grist Mill State Park is located at 5512 Mount Vernon Memorial Highway (State Route 235), 2.5 miles west of Mount Vernon, near the intersection of U.S. 1 (Richmond Highway).*

# WOODLAWN PLANTATION

Woodlawn Plantation was created by George Washington's will. He gave two thousand acres—a quarter of his Mount Vernon estate—to his granddaughter, Nelly Custis, and her husband, Lawrence Lewis, Washington's nephew. Their inheritance included the gristmill and distillery. The couple hired William Thornton, the first architect of the U.S. Capitol, to design the house, which was built from 1800 to 1805. Woodlawn was a plantation, and many slaves toiled here. The plantation was built along Dogue Creek and had a view of the creek's wide channel as it entered the Potomac. The National Trust for Historic Preservation acquired Woodlawn in 1952 as its very first property. Today, 126 acres remain of the property. In addition to the house, Woodlawn Plantation has gardens to browse.

## *The Pope Leighey House*

Frank Lloyd Wright designed the Falls Church, Virginia home for Loren Pope in 1940. Pope was a copy editor at the *Washington Evening Star* and had asked Wright to build one of his "Usonian" homes, designed for people of moderate incomes. Pope sold it in 1946 to Margaret Leighey, who donated it to the National Trust for Historic Preservation in 1964 but continued to live in it. The next year, the trust moved the house from Falls Church to Woodlawn Plantation, as it lay in the path of Interstate 66, then under construction.

*How to get there: Woodlawn Plantation is located at the intersection of U.S. Route 1 (Richmond Highway) and Route 235, three miles west of Mount Vernon.*

## BELVOIR

William Fairfax, who managed the Northern Neck Propriety for his cousin, Lord Thomas Fairfax, built the Belvoir mansion in 1741 and lived there until his death in 1757. This was a colonial plantation with a Georgian manor house set on a steep bluff over the Potomac. Lord Fairfax lived there as well for three years until he moved to Greenway Court near Winchester in 1751, at the center of his Northern Neck holdings.

William was a powerful person, serving in the House of Burgesses and as president of the King's Council of Virginia. He pressed the commonwealth to create Fairfax County in 1742. He became a close friend of his Mount Vernon neighbor, the young George Washington. Fairfax hired sixteen-year-old Washington to survey Fairfax's land for subdivision in 1748. George became lifelong friends with Fairfax's son, George William, and his wife, Sally, with whom George was infatuated.

William Fairfax and his second wife, Deborah, are buried at the Fairfax grave near the manor house, along with two of the Fairfax sons. The site is marked with an obelisk erected in 1924. George William Fairfax inherited Belvoir from his father but left for England in 1773. George Washington purchased many of the house's furnishings a year later. Rented to a local minister, the mansion burned down in 1783, and the estate never recovered.

During World War I, the U.S. Army established Camp A.A. Humphreys around the Belvoir estate and then renamed it Fort Belvoir in 1935. It became the main training camp for army engineers. There isn't much left of the Belvoir mansion other than foundation stones. A one-mile interpreted trail takes you to the Belvoir ruins and the Fairfax grave site and along steep bluffs overlooking the Potomac with magnificent views.

## *The Battle of White House*

What remained of the burned Belvoir mansion was destroyed in September 1814 after the British raid on Washington. As a Royal Navy squadron retired down the Potomac from occupying Alexandria, U.S. Navy captain David Porter set up batteries on bluffs over the Potomac on grounds near Ferdinando Fairfax's home, known as White House. Porter shelled the fleet for five days. The British finally silenced the guns, but not before Belvoir's remnants were destroyed.

*How to get there: Fort Belvoir is fifteen miles south of Washington, D.C., on U.S. 1. Visitors must enter through Tully Gate. Proceed down Gunston Road and then turn left on Twenty-third Street and right on Forney Loop and proceed into the Fairfax Village development. Park at the Fairfax Village Neighborhood Center, where the Belvoir ruins trail begins.*

# POHICK CHURCH

Established in 1732, Pohick Church was George Washington's local congregation, and he was elected vestryman in 1762. From 1769 to 1774, the Anglican parish constructed a new church, which we see today. It is a handsome, simple brick Georgian building with no steeple or bell tower. The pews inside are uniquely set up in boxes. This reflects the society of the eighteenth-century colonial elite, where families owned their pews and sat together. There was also a practical reason: during winter, people brought their own source of heat and huddled together to stay warm.

George Washington and George Mason worshipped at Pohick Church, a simple, elegant structure. *Library of Congress.*

George Washington was a vestryman for twenty-three years at Pohick Church, though he did not attend much after 1775 because of the Revolution. George Fairfax, son George William and George Mason were also members, as the church sat roughly halfway between their estates (Belvoir and Gunston Hall, respectively). During the Civil War, Union troops used the church's wooden structures for firewood. Federal forces operated an observation balloon at the church, and there they watched the Confederates withdraw from their defensive lines around Manassas in March 1862. There is a pleasant cemetery adjacent to Pohick Church, and headstones in the churchyard are a who's who of colonial Virginia. The church is today an active congregation and not a museum.

*How to get there: Pohick Church sits on U.S. 1 (Richmond Highway), just west of Fort Belvoir at Telegraph Road.*

# GUNSTON HALL AND MASON NECK

George Mason (1725–1792) began building an attractive Georgian home on the boot-shaped peninsula now known as Mason Neck in 1755. He named it Gunston Hall. Mason moved into the house in 1758. Richard Blackburn was the architect; he also designed Mount Vernon and Rippon Lodge.

When the American Revolution began in 1776, Mason was called to Williamsburg, the capital of Virginia. He helped draft the state's new constitution and wrote the Virginia Declaration of Rights. This became the model for Thomas Jefferson's Declaration of Independence later that year. Though he attended the Constitutional Convention in 1787, he refused to sign the U.S. Constitution, as it did not include a Bill of Rights. That was added later.

Yes, Mason was a slaveholder who paradoxically was dedicated to the cause of freedom. It is a challenge to reconcile this basic fact. Many of our beloved Founding Fathers from the South—George Washington, Thomas Jefferson and George Mason—were slaveholders. Freedom apparently was not for everyone.

Gunston Hall was once a 5,500-acre plantation where ninety African American slaves and twenty indentured servants toiled, growing corn, tobacco and wheat. Gunston Hall and 550 acres were donated to the Commonwealth of Virginia in 1949. Considered a mansion in its time, the house is beautiful but not extravagant, and it is meticulously restored. The grounds also include a dairy, a kitchen, a laundry, a schoolyard and a smokehouse, as well as interpretive signs detailing the lives of the slaves who worked this plantation. The boxwood garden dates from about 1760. A lovely lane of magnolia trees leads to the house. George Mason and members of his family are buried at the family cemetery.

Visitors often arrived by boat. The house once had a fine view of the Potomac, as it sits half a mile uphill. However, the farmland around the mansion has become forest, so the view has disappeared. Being a gentleman planter, Mason exported many of his goods, especially tobacco. He built a small wharf. Mason used the creek through his property as a canal for small boats to row out to merchant vessels anchored in Gunston Cove. He also maintained a deer park for his household consumption.

Gunston Hall has a worthwhile hike down to the Potomac, the Barn Wharf Trail, which begins next to the house. Here the river is calm, lapping gently at your feet. The Maryland side is almost two miles away and is lushly forested. To return, simply retrace your steps up the hill.

*How to get there: Take I-95 to Lorton and then follow the signs for Gunston Hall. It is just down Gunston Road from Pohick Bay Regional Park.*

## Elizabeth Hartwell Mason Neck National Wildlife Refuge

Mason Neck rivals Great Falls and Harpers Ferry for its sheer abundance of natural beauty, wildlife and walking and cycling trails along the Potomac River. It is a peninsula shaped like a boot, surrounded by Belmont and Occoquan Bay to the west, Gunston Cove to the east and the Potomac to the south. It is best known as a 6,400-acre nature preserve with one of the largest freshwater marshes on the Potomac—the 250-acre Great Marsh—and as a refuge for more than two hundred species of birds, including the bald eagle.

Mason Neck National Wildlife Refuge is a 2,277-acre refuge established in 1969 as the first sanctuary in the country to protect the bald eagle. It is named after Elizabeth Hartwell, the local "eagle lady" who tirelessly worked to preserve eagle habitat on the peninsula. The national bird made a remarkable comeback in the Potomac region after the United States banned the pesticide DDT in 1973.

The national wildlife refuge has two main walking trails: the Great Marsh Trail and the Woodmarsh Trail. The Great Marsh Trail is a 1.5-mile round-trip along a flat, paved trail that leads to an overlook above the Great Marsh. The trail begins on the east side of the refuge on Gunston Road.

The Woodmarsh Trail is two to three miles through the "arch" of the boot that is Mason Neck. The trail is flat and very easy and can be done in an hour. It begins on High Point Road, and you'll walk a mile to reach Eagle Point overlooking the Great Marsh. You can then backtrack to your car or continue to the west to a circular "fan" of trails: Hickory Pass and the Fern Trail. The area is especially spectacular in fall as the hardwood forests change color. Eagles are easiest to spot in winter, when the leaves are gone and the eagles are incubating their eggs.

*How to get there: From Washington, D.C., drive I-95 South. Take Exit 163 (Lorton/ Gunston Hall) and follow the signs. Take a right onto U.S. 1 and then a left on State Route 242 (Gunston Road). Take a right on High Point Road into the refuge.*

## Pohick Bay Regional Park

There are two additional recreation areas on Mason Neck: Pohick Bay Regional Park and Mason Neck State Park. Pohick Creek flows into Pohick Bay, which forms the northern border of Pohick Bay Regional Park. There are several color-coded short trails in the park. The best way to explore the water is by canoe, which can be rented through the park. Guided tours with a naturalist are available.

With its sandy bottom and swift current, Pohick Creek is shallow in most places. Chemicals, nutrients and silt pass down the creek and are filtered in the bay's tidal marsh. Mud flats are exposed at low tide. Many animals make this their home. Beavers build their houses and dams along the creek. A dozen types of fish migrate up the creek to spawn, including shad, perch and herring. Catfish live in the creek year round. Ospreys catch fish and then are chased by bald eagles, which try to steal their prize. Both birds can be seen roosting high in trees along the banks.

*How to get there: From Washington, D.C., take I-95 South. Take Exit 163 (Lorton/ Gunston Hall) and follow the signs. Take a right onto U.S. 1, then a left on State Route 242 (Gunston Road). Take a left on Pohick Bay Drive and follow the signs to the visitor center.*

## Mason Neck State Park

Mason Neck State Park lies on the western or "toe" side of Mason Neck. It borders Belmont Bay to the northwest. There are four easy hiking trails in the park: Beach Trail, Kane's Creek, Wilson Spring and Bay View. They total three miles and all intersect. The Kane's Creek Trail ends at an eagle blind, the best place to spot a passing bald eagle.

Another way to experience Mason Neck State Park is on a guided canoe trip. These take you up Kane's Creek (with a paddle, of course). The creek is a wide, shallow channel where wild rice grows in abundance, attracting Canada geese. You are bound to spot bald eagles, kingfishers and ospreys. You may even see a beaver house along the banks.

*How to get there: From Washington, D.C., drive I-95 South. Take Exit 163 (Lorton/ Gunston Hall) and follow the signs. Take a right onto U.S. 1 and then a left on State Route 242 (Gunston Road). Take a right on High Point Road and follow this to the state park.*

## The Return of the Bald Eagle

Bald eagles, our national bird, live throughout the Potomac River Valley. The Chesapeake Bay and James and Rappahannock Rivers also provide ideal eagle habitats. Eagles prefer to nest in high trees along shorelines to catch fish.

There were as many as 100,000 bald eagle nesting pairs in the continental United States when European settlers first arrived. Their habitat gradually disappeared through development and hunting. In 1940, Congress passed the Bald and Golden Eagle Protection Act, making it a crime to kill the bird or disturb its nest. But an even deadlier threat appeared through DDT, a pesticide used to fight mosquitoes. It made the eagles lay thin-shelled eggs that were easily crushed. Few eaglets were born, and the population spiraled downward. By 1963, only 417 pairs survived in the continental United States. Though Mason Neck was set aside in 1969 as a bald eagle preserve, there were only 72 nesting pairs left in Maryland and Virginia. The bird was heading toward extinction.

The Environmental Protection Agency banned the use of DDT in 1972, and the following year, the bald eagle was placed on the Endangered Species List. This also protected the eagle's waterfront habitat. The population slowly began to recover, reaching one thousand nesting pairs nationwide by 1980 and then dramatically rising after lead shot for hunters was phased out in 1991, which eliminated lead poisoning in birds (eagles are scavengers and often eat wounded or dead waterfowl like ducks).

Eagles made such a strong recovery in the Washington area that their nesting sites became more crowded—and fights broke out over preferred habitat. In 2000, a bald eagle chick was hatched in Southeast Washington land near Bolling Air Force Base. This was the first eagle born in the district

Two bald eagles perched in a tree above the Accokeek Creek Site in Piscataway Park. *Garrett Peck.*

in more than a half century, showing that eagles will settle closer to urban areas than was previously believed.

With its population on the rebound and its habitat protected, the bald eagle was removed from the Endangered Species List in 2007. The bird has also adapted to urban and semiurban environments, building nests within a stone's throw of the Woodrow Wilson Bridge and fishing in the warm waters below the Blue Plains sewage treatment plant.

Bald eagles are thriving on Mason Neck, an ideal environment with its tall hardwood trees and extensive waterfront along fish-filled streams. The bald eagle can live up to thirty years; they can reach fourteen pounds and have a wingspan of eight feet. Eagles mate after their fourth year, which is when they reach maturity and their heads turn from brown to white. A pair will occupy the same treetop nest, raising two to three eaglets each year. Eagles are especially susceptible to disturbance while they are incubating eggs in winter. Nesting areas are often cordoned off so as not to disturb the birds.

The rebound of the bald eagle from the brink of extinction to a thriving population is a remarkable story. Development still poses a threat to its habitat as the human population expands and people settle along the waterfront, the eagle's ideal habitat.

*How to get there: Mason Neck is twenty miles south of Washington near Lorton. From Washington, drive I-95 South. Take Exit 163 (Lorton/Gunston Hall) and follow the signs. Take a right onto U.S. 1 and then a left on State Route 242 (Gunston Road). Continue past Pohick Bay Regional Park and then Gunston Hall. Look for the signs on the right for Mason Neck State Park, which is on High Point Road.*

# Occoquan Bay National Wildlife Refuge

Directly on Belmont and Occoquan Bays and west of Mason Neck is the Occoquan Bay National Wildlife Refuge. Formerly a farm, this 644-acre preserve was the U.S. Army's East Coast Radio Transmitting Station from 1950 to 1994. It housed the Harry Diamond Laboratories, where the U.S. Army studied simulated nuclear blasts. After the Cold War ended, the military no longer needed the station, and in 1998, it became a national wildlife refuge. The refuge is covered in pristine grasslands and is a key stopover for migrating birds. Walking paths crisscross the refuge and traverse the shoreline. A half-mile walk down Fox Road leads you to a gazebo with views of the Potomac and Featherstone and Freestone Points downriver. Two miles up the Occoquan River is the historic town of Occoquan, a former tobacco port.

*How to get there: Occoquan Bay National Wildlife Refuse is twenty miles south of Washington on U.S. 1.*

## RIPPON LODGE HISTORIC SITE

Rippon Lodge is the oldest surviving colonial house on the Potomac. It was built in 1747 (not 1725 as many signs say) on a tobacco and wheat plantation that Richard Blackburn acquired from Lord Thomas Fairfax. An English immigrant and carpenter, Blackburn was the architect for the house and also designed Mount Vernon and Gunston Hall. George Washington was a visitor, and Colonel Thomas Blackburn, the builder's son, was Washington's aide-de-camp during the War of Independence.

In 1924, Judge Wade Ellis purchased the property and greatly expanded the house. Its next owner was Admiral Richard Blackburn Black, who bought the property in 1952. Prince William County purchased the house from Black's daughter in 2000 and opened it to the public. Rippon Lodge now sits on forty acres on a bluff overlooking the Potomac and Neabsco Creek, the only acreage remaining to this plantation, surrounded by suburbia and the strip mall–lined Route 1.

*How to get there: Rippon Lodge Historic Site is at 15520 Blackburn Road in Woodbridge, Virginia.*

# THE CIVIL WAR ON THE LOWER POTOMAC

After his victory at the First Battle of Manassas on July 21, 1861, Confederate general Joseph E. Johnston extended his defensive lines across northern Virginia from Leesburg to the Occoquan River. The Confederates constructed artillery batteries along the Potomac below the Occoquan, about thirty miles south of Washington. Six miles of batteries totaling thirty-seven heavy guns created a gauntlet for the Rebels to halt Union commerce and troop movements on the river. The Confederates secretly established their batteries on points jutting into the river—Freestone Point, Cockpit Point, Shipping Point (now part of Quantico) and Evansport.

Meanwhile, the Federal's powerful Potomac Flotilla prevented the Confederates from using the river. It shut down the nightly traffic of small boats that brought supplies from southern Maryland to Virginia. What few vessels the Confederates had were trapped in creeks—they didn't dare sail on the river. On October 11, 1861, a small group of Federal sailors rowed into Quantico Creek under the cover of darkness and burned the schooner *Martha Washington.*

Four days after the raid, the Confederates revealed their batteries, opening fire on the Union ships *Pocahontas* and *Seminole*. The five-month blockade of the Potomac had begun. However, this was minimally effective: Union shipping was rerouted to Baltimore, and the B&O Railroad supplied the capital. The railroad kept the city alive during the first year of the Civil War.

On November 11, 1861, the United States launched an aerial reconnaissance balloon, the *Constitution*, to map the Confederate batteries.

It was launched from a boat anchored in the Potomac, the *G.W. Parke Custis*. The balloon was later moved inland to observe the Confederate lines along the Occoquan River.

In January 1862, the heavily armed USS *Pensacola* ran the blockade. Once the Federals realized that Confederate fire was inaccurate, they started sailing ships past the gauntlet at night. Few were hit, and not a single ship was lost, though the Confederates fired some five thousand shots. The Confederates finally abandoned the batteries on March 8 when they pulled back behind the Rappahannock River. Today, the best place to see the remains of the Confederate Potomac batteries is in Leesylvania State Park.

# LEESYLVANIA STATE PARK

Leesylvania State Park is on a peninsula between Neabsco Creek to the north, Powell's Creek to the south and the Potomac to the east. Leesylvania means "Lee's Woods." It was a Lee family plantation and was later owned by Colonel John Fairfax. Tobacco was grown here until the soil degraded, and it served as a slave-driven plantation until emancipation.

A philanthropist, Daniel K. Ludwig, ceded the two-thousand-acre peninsula to Virginia in 1978, and it formally became a park in 1989. Today, the park is bisected by CSX railroad tracks, which have cut through Leesylvania since 1872. The park has a lengthy Potomac shoreline, with a large boat launch. This is particularly popular with fishers and boaters. There are also extensive picnic facilities, barbecue grills, a sandy beach, public restrooms and a visitor center.

There are four hikes in Leesylvania State Park, and each offers something different. The Potomac Heritage Trail is a continuation of the statewide trail network; Powell's Creek Trail is the most natural; Bushey Point Trail offers fine views of the Potomac; and Lee's Woods Trail is the most historic. All four are shaded and pleasant on a hot day. Bring insect repellent.

## *Lee's Woods Trail*

The two-mile Lee's Woods Trail is simply one of the best trails on the Potomac for its history and natural beauty, particularly in autumn after the leaves have fallen. The trail begins at an amphitheater built from the remains of a duck club that stood until 1985. A series of steps climb to reach a bluff known as Freestone Point. There you'll see the northernmost of the artillery batteries that Confederates erected along the Potomac in 1861 to blockade the river. It has a fine view of the river.

The trail continues west past views of the Potomac and Occoquan Bay and through a forest of paw paw trees. It then reaches the remains of the Fairfax House, built about 1803. Henry Fairfax purchased the two-thousand-acre Lee plantation in 1825. His son, Colonel John Walter Fairfax, inherited the property in 1847. Fairfax rebuilt the house in 1877, but it burned down shortly after his death in 1908. The remains include the chimney, as well as foundations of the barn, house and kitchen.

The Lee House site marks about the halfway point of the trail. It now resides in a second-growth forest, but at the time it was in the middle of a tobacco plantation worked by at least fifty slaves. Henry Lee II and his wife, Lucy, had eight children born here; among them were the Revolutionary War hero Henry "Light Horse Harry" Lee III, the father of Robert E. Lee. Henry died in 1787, and the house burned down in about 1790. Henry and Lucy Lee were buried at the Lee family cemetery, as were Henry and Elizabeth Fairfax, at the top of the ridge.

*Hot to get there: Leesylvania is thirty miles south of Washington, D.C., on Interstate 95 South. Take Exit 156 and follow the signs to Leesylvania State Park. Drive south on U.S. 1 and then turn left on Neabsco Road.*

## Public Quarry at Government Island

Near the town of Aquia was a freestone (sandstone) quarry used for more than two centuries, starting about 1694—and perhaps as long as ten thousand years ago by natives. Pierre L'Enfant purchased the quarry for the federal government in 1791 to provide stone for the new nation's capital. Scottish stonemasons and African slaves once worked here. Stone blocks were transported by ship to Washington, D.C.

The Public Quarry provided Aquia Creek sandstone for Washington's boundary stones, the White House, U.S. Capitol, U.S. Treasury building, Old Patent Office, the four Georgetown locks on the C&O Canal, tombstones at Congressional Cemetery and numerous other public buildings. George Mason used Aquia sandstone at Gunston Hall, and Washington used it for the walkways at Mount Vernon. The quarry may have also provided stone for historic Aquia Episcopal Church nearby, built in 1751–57 (during the

Pierre L'Enfant purchased the Public Quarry on Government Island for public buildings in Washington, D.C. It is now a park in Stafford County, Virginia. *Garrett Peck.*

Civil War, Confederate and Union troops etched graffiti on the church's cornerstones and quoins). The quarry was abandoned when the Capitol was completed in 1829.

Stafford County opened Government Island as a park in 2010. A raised wooden walkway, part of a 1.5-mile interpretive trail, leads you over wetlands to the "island"—really a peninsula set on Austin Run and Aquia Creek. Numerous quarries dot the landscape, and chisel marks are clearly visible. This is also a popular spot for bird watching.

*How to get there: Government Island is at 191 Coal Landing Road in Stafford, Virginia. Aquia Episcopal Church is at 2938 Jefferson Davis Highway (U.S. 1) in Stafford, about three miles northwest of Government Island.*

## AQUIA LANDING

It may not look like much today, but Aquia Landing was once part of the Underground Railroad and a key supply link for the Union Army of the Potomac during the Civil War. It sits at the mouth of Aquia Creek and the Potomac, northeast of Fredericksburg.

To get from Washington to Richmond in the mid-1800s, travelers boarded a Washington & Fredericksburg Steamboat Company steamer (renamed the Potomac Steamboat Company in 1855) at Washington's waterfront that took them to Aquia Landing. There they would disembark and take the Richmond, Fredericksburg and Potomac Railroad, which opened in 1842. This shortened travel between the two cities to nine hours. Escaped slaves such as William and Ellen Craft and Henry "Box" Brown passed through Aquia Landing on the Underground Railroad.

Early in the Civil War, the Confederates erected a three-gun battery next to the wharf to protect the railroad terminus; however, the channel was too wide for Confederate artillery to disrupt shipping on the Potomac. The Army of the Potomac captured the abandoned battery in March 1862 and then used Aquia Landing as a main supply point during the Fredericksburg and Chancellorsville Campaigns. They brought in supplies from the wharf over the railroad, which is now the road leading into the park.

Some ten thousand escaped slaves fled from plantations and headed north during the war via Aquia Landing. It earned the nickname as the "gateway to freedom." Union forces abandoned Aquia Landing during the Gettysburg Campaign, and Confederates destroyed the depot. In 1872, the railroad was extended from Fredericksburg directly to Washington, ending the need for steamship travel.

Just north of Aquia Creek is Widewater State Park, 1,100 wooded acres that Virginia preserved in 2007. Not far south of Aquia Landing is

Civil War photographer Alexander Gardner produced this 1863 photo of Aquia Landing, a key Union supply point during the war. *Library of Congress.*

the Crow's Nest, a pristine 3,200-acre peninsula between Accokeek and Potomac Creeks. It is home to large tidal marshes, hardware forests and one of the largest heron colonies in the Chesapeake region. In 2009, Virginia and Stafford County acquired most of the land for a state park, Crow's Nest Natural Area Preserve.

*How to get there: Aquia Landing Beach Park is at 2846 Brooke Road in Stafford, Virginia.*

# THE NORTHERN NECK

The Northern Neck is the peninsula between the Potomac and Rappahannock Rivers. It is a beautiful region—geographic isolation has left it largely covered in hardwood forests, the tobacco-growing plantation era having died two centuries ago. Visitors find creeks and peaceful inlets, chalky cliffs that yield ancient sharks' teeth and a thriving bald eagle population in Caledon Natural Area State Park. The Potomac is brackish and smells of the sea. The Governor Harry M. Nice Bridge (U.S. Route 301) connects Virginia to Maryland at Dahlgren, which is the last crossing point over the river.

The Northern Neck is some of the oldest-settled land along the Potomac, dating to the 1600s. In colonial times, the Northern Neck was vastly greater in size: it represented all of Lord Thomas Fairfax's landholdings, all of northern Virginia to the Fairfax Stone in West Virginia. This was about a quarter of the state. Three presidents were born on the peninsula: George Washington, James Madison and James Monroe. In addition, Robert E. Lee was born at his family's ancestral home, Stratford Hall.

## COLONIAL BEACH

Colonial Beach is a sleepy beach town that was once a hot spot for gambling known as the "Las Vegas on the Potomac." Set on a peninsula curving into the river, the town took advantage of Maryland's gambling laws, building several casinos on piers in the river in the 1950s. Since the Potomac is entirely in Maryland, the casinos didn't violate Virginia law. Maryland outlawed casinos operating off the Virginia shore in 1959, shutting down the casinos. A fire burned them to the waterline in the 1960s.

The town today has just one pier, Municipal Pier, many seafood restaurants and a long beach. Many residents travel through town on golf carts. The Riverboat on the Potomac hosts off-track betting, just a few steps into Maryland on the river. President James Monroe was born just south of Colonial Beach, and there is a marker on Route 205.

*How to get there: Colonial Beach is sixty-five miles from Washington, D.C., either by Interstate 95 to Fredericksburg and then Route 3 East or by U.S. 301 through Maryland.*

## George Washington Birthplace National Monument

The first president of the United States, George Washington, was born at this modest plantation on February 22, 1732. Popes Creek provided an outlet to the Potomac, connecting with ships to take the plantation's crops to Europe. Washington only lived there for his first four years. The house burned down on Christmas 1779; only its foundations are visible now. Before the property was excavated, the Memorial House was built in 1931 for the bicentennial of Washington's birth, though it was a lot nicer than the actual house. Five generations of Washingtons are buried at the family cemetery. Today, the National Park Service administers 538 acres of the plantation, using farming practices from colonial times.

*How to get there: George Washington Birthplace is at 1732 Popes Creek Road, thirty-eight miles east of Fredericksburg on State Route 3.*

## Westmoreland State Park

Virginia bought the 1,311 acres in 1933 that became Westmoreland State Park. It was once the Cliffts Plantation, part of Stratford Hall. The mile-long Big Meadow Trail leads to Fossil Beach. Much of the park's shoreline are the 150-foot-high Horsehead Cliffs, chalky cliffs that are retreating, revealing many fossils from the Miocene epoch some 17 million years ago, when this was the bottom of the ocean and a rich hunting ground.

*How to get there: Westmoreland State Park is at 1650 State Park Road in Montross, Virginia.*

# STRATFORD HALL

Stratford Hall was built starting about 1738 by Thomas Lee and became the Lee family home for four generations. The grand brick mansion was at the center of a large tobacco plantation on which 220 indentured servants and slaves toiled, a culture that declined by the end of the century from slash-and-burn agriculture.

The Lees were one of Virginia's most prominent families. Two Lee brothers, Francis Lightfoot Lee and Richard Henry Lee, signed the Declaration of Independence. And here Robert E. Lee was born in 1807. The future general of the Confederacy was the son of Henry "Light Horse Harry" Lee, a distant cousin to this branch of the family. Henry was a

Stratford Hall was the Lee family home for four generations. Robert E. Lee was born there in 1807. *Garrett Peck.*

brilliant tactician in the War of Independence but a poor businessman who ended up in debtor's prison twice. Before little Robert was even four, his family left Stratford Hall for a more modest home in Alexandria, where he grew up. The Lee family lost the property in the 1820s.

Today, Stratford Hall is owned by the Robert E. Lee Memorial Association. It has carefully restored the house, gardens and outbuildings on the 1,900-acre park and operates a visitor center. There are cabins for overnight guests and nature trails run through the grounds. One trail leads to the Potomac shoreline, where fossils like Miocene epoch sharks' teeth can be found in the chalky cliffs.

*How to get there: Stratford Hall is located at 483 Great House Road in Stratford, Virginia, forty-five minutes east of Fredericksburg.*

# THE PISCATAWAY NATION

The Piscataways were the most powerful Indian tribe along Maryland's Potomac shore, though they lost their power as Europeans settled on their land. This was the tribe the St. Mary's settlement dealt with, and many streams and towns along the lower Potomac bear Piscataway names. Though the Piscataways are not federally recognized, the tribe maintains a presence along the river.

The historic tobacco-growing region begins in Prince George's County. Dominated by tobacco farming for three centuries, the county has transformed into a Washington suburb and bedroom community. Prince George's shoreline provided the defense against seaborne invaders who might sail up the Potomac to attack Washington. Two major nineteenth-century forts still exist along the river, Fort Foote and Fort Washington.

## OXON HILL

Oxon Cove Park is a prominent piece of National Park Service property between the Woodrow Wilson Bridge, the Capitol Beltway and Blue Plains. Its main feature is Oxon Hill Farm, a working farm overlooking Oxon Cove that is open to visitors and school groups. Nearly two dozen buildings crowd this former tobacco plantation, the oldest of which was the White Farm House, also known as Mount Welby. An Irish immigrant, Dr. Samuel DeButts, built the house in 1805 and bought 250 acres from Oxon Hill

Manor. Saint Elizabeths Hospital acquired the farm in 1891 to supply food for its mentally ill patients. The property has two main walking paths: the short Woodlot Trail through the forest and the 1.6-mile Hiker/Biker Trail that leads to Oxon Cove.

## Oxon Hill Manor

Just south of the Capitol Beltway, Oxon Hill Manor is a grand Georgian mansion built in 1928 with a remarkable view of the Potomac. President Franklin Roosevelt was a frequent visitor to the home's owner, Sumner Welles. The first manor was built in 1711 by Thomas Addison but burned down in 1895. John Hanson, the first president of the Continental Congress under the Articles of Confederation, visited the mansion often and died there in 1783. The home is now administered by Prince George's County and used for events such as weddings.

*How to get there: Oxon Hill Farm is immediately north of the Woodrow Wilson Bridge and the Capitol Beltway (Interstate 495). Oxon Hill Manor is at 6901 Oxon Hill Road in Oxon Hill, Maryland.*

## FORT FOOTE PARK

Fort Washington was the primary defense for the nation's capital along the Potomac, but during the Civil War, that fort was considered too far to protect the city, in part because the surrounding population was pro-Confederacy. In 1863, Union forces built Fort Foote on a hundred-foot bluff that was closer to Washington. This was the southernmost and largest of the sixty-eight forts that ringed the capital during the war. Fort Foote is remarkably intact for an earthen fortification. Two fifteen-inch smoothbore Rodman guns stand guard on the river—they were too heavy to remove. These could hurl a 434-pound ball three miles.

*How to get there: Fort Foote is one mile south of National Harbor. From Oxon Hill Road, turn right on Fort Foote Road and follow to the park.*

Two enormous fifteen-inch Rodman guns stand guard over the Potomac at Fort Foote. *Garrett Peck.*

## HARMONY HALL

Harmony Hall, a fine Georgian plantation manor, was built in the 1720s above Broad Creek. The house sits on sixty-five acres of National Park Service land but is not currently open to the public. At the shoreline, you'll find ruins of the Lyles House, known for most of its history as Want Water and built as early as the 1690s. Nearby is a man-made canal to help load tobacco on ships for England. Colonel William Lyles owned both Harmony Hall and Want Water. He was a friend of George Washington's, and lore has it that Washington visited Lyles there numerous times and that they worshiped together at St. John's Church (9801 Livingston Road) half a mile north. Lyles died in 1815 and is buried at the church.

*How to get there: Harmony Hall is at 10511 Livingston Road in Silesia, Maryland.*

## FORT WASHINGTON NATIONAL PARK

Shortly after Washington, D.C., was established, the War Department realized that the new capital was vulnerable to attack from the Potomac. It built Fort Warburton on a high bluff ten miles south of the city in 1808. Two days after the British burned Washington during the War of 1812, a Royal Navy squadron sailed up the river on August 26, 1814. The garrison blew up the magazine without firing a shot and fled. The next day, the British battered the fort and then passed by to occupy Alexandria.

Built in 1824, Fort Washington protected the nation's capital and is now a national park. *Garrett Peck.*

The military rebuilt the fort from 1820 to 1824 as a huge masonry structure and renamed it Fort Washington. It sits directly across the river from Fort Hunt, Virginia. These were the two primary fortifications protecting the capital from enemy ships sailing up the Potomac.

Fort Washington is intact and impressive to visit. Standing atop the parapet, you can see the commanding military position that this site held. As technology changed, so did the fort: three tiers of defenses were built, including eight concrete batteries added in 1896 to fight armored warships. Fort Washington was deactivated in 1946. Besides the walking tour through the masonry fort, the park offers a three-mile ring trail past the lighthouse and many of the later fortifications and through the riparian forest along Piscataway Creek. Canoes and kayaks can be rented at the adjacent Fort Washington Marina.

*How to get there: Fort Washington is eight miles south of the Capitol Beltway (I-495) in Fort Washington, Maryland. From Indian Head Highway, take Livingston Road and then follow Fort Washington Road to the park.*

# Piscataway Park

Piscataway Park is home to one of the most significant Indian archaeological finds along the Potomac: the Accokeek Creek Site. The Piscataway Indians and their ancestors occupied the site for thousands of years. This was a large, seasonally occupied stockade village called Moyaone (pronounced *moy-own*). The tribe considers the site sacred, as it was used for burials, and the Piscataways still use the site ceremonially. Alice Ferguson led the excavations at Moyaone in the 1930s and 1940s. Numerous ossuaries were uncovered; a red cedar tree planted in 1976 marks one of them.

Piscataway Park is a five-thousand-acre national park that covers six miles of Potomac shoreline. It was established in 1961 with the consent of the Piscataway Indians and county residents who sought to protect this pristine watershed from development. It is directly across from Mount Vernon, with views of the mansion from almost everywhere along the shoreline.

Moyaone is located off Bryan Point Road down a gravel road about eight hundred feet before the National Colonial Farm turnoff. A short walk leads to a boardwalk over Accokeek Creek, which then dead-ends at the site. In 2010, the Living Shoreline project built up the riverbank with stones to prevent erosion. Beyond the national park boundaries, Moyaone Reserve easements protect the Mount Vernon viewshed.

Piscataway Park has several living history sites. The National Colonial Farm was established in 1957 to re-create a tobacco farm from the 1770s. Several miles of interpreted trails traverse the farm, as well as its fields, forests and wetlands. The Hard Bargain Farm nearby is a reservations-only working farm for school groups.

On the western side of Piscataway Park is Marshall Hall, built in 1690 by William Marshall. A ferry to Virginia was established there in 1745. The property eventually became part of Washington's Union Farm. There isn't much to see other than the stabilized brick ruins of the house and the Marshall family cemetery. An amusement park was on this location in the 1950s and 1960s. Fishing is popular, and there are several boat launches in Piscataway Park.

*How to get there: Piscataway Park is ten miles south of the Capitol Beltway (I-495) near Indian Head Highway. The National Colonial Farm is at 3400 Bryan Point Road in Accokeek. Marshall Hall Road (Route 227) leads to Marshall Hall.*

# CHAPMAN STATE PARK

Nathaniel Chapman bought the land for a riverside plantation in 1750, and these grounds remained in the family until 1914. At the center of the park is a grand mansion called Mount Aventine, built about 1840, with a jaw-dropping view of the Potomac. The estate was a Hungarian thoroughbred horse farm in the late twentieth century before becoming a state park in 1998.

Much of the park is heavily wooded, but these vary significantly in habitat. The 0.6-mile Potomac River Trail connects Chapman Landing Road to the mansion and then continues to the river. The 0.7-mile Marsh Trail leads to a scrubby marsh, while the 1.0-mile Coastal Woodlands Trail threads through an oak forest and along the Potomac shore.

The park is adjacent to the town of Indian Head, a peninsula between the Potomac and Mattawoman Creek. The peninsula, which is largely a naval base, marks the beginning of the Indian Head Rail Trail. This thirteen-mile rails-to-trails path connects to White Plains.

*How to get there: Mount Aventine is located at 3452 Ferry Place in Indian Head, Maryland.*

# GENERAL SMALLWOOD STATE PARK

General William Smallwood was the highest-ranking Marylander during the American Revolution. Part of the planter class, he owned a tobacco plantation overlooking Mattawoman Creek. His home was known as the Retreat House. Smallwood later served as governor of Maryland from 1785 to 1788 and helped negotiate the Mount Vernon Compact. When the bachelor Smallwood died in 1792, his sister inherited the plantation and fifty-six slaves.

The Retreat House was rebuilt in 1958 on the original foundations, along with a tobacco barn and other structures, and became the core of 628-acre General Smallwood State Park. The house is open for tours from May to September. The park has extensive recreational facilities, including the Sweden Point Marina and campgrounds. A two-mile loop, the General's Walk Foot Trail, passes through the park's forests and streams.

*How to get there: General Smallwood State Park is seven miles south of Indian Head on Maryland Route 224.*

# Mallows Bay Ship Graveyard

Mallows Bay is one of the most fascinating finds on the Potomac that you've likely never heard of. This small park contains the graves of more than 230 ships sunk in the river. Almost 90 of them were poorly constructed steamships built during World War I; in 1925, they were burned and scuttled in the bay. Bethlehem Steel then built a salvage basin to recover metal from the abandoned ships. The ships form a reef that hosts an array of wildlife. It is popular to canoe or kayak among the ship ruins. A 0.8-mile trail loops around Mallows Bay Park and the salvage basin.

*How to get there: Mallows Bay Park is at 1440 Wilson Landing Road in Nanjemoy, Maryland.*

# Purse State Park

Less than three miles south of Mallows Bay is Purse State Park, an isolated tract on the Potomac that is home to bald eagles and thick woods. A short walk leads to twenty-foot cliffs along the river that steadily erode. Fossils such as sharks' teeth often fall from the cliffs, revealing themselves at low tide. These are from the Paleocene epoch, some 50 to 60 million years ago, when this area was underwater.

*How to get there: Purse State Park is on Maryland Route 224 in Nanjemoy.*

# CATHOLIC BEGINNINGS AT THE RIVER'S END

King Charles I of England gave George Calvert, a Catholic convert and commoner who was knighted as the first Lord Baltimore, a land grant that included the Potomac River. By the time the king sealed the charter on June 20, 1632, Calvert had died. His oldest son, Cecil, became second Lord Baltimore, and although he never visited the New World, he sent his brother, Leonard, to establish the Potomac colony that their father had dreamed about, one that would be tolerant to both Catholics and Protestants. In 1634, Leonard Calvert led 140 English Catholic settlers to *Terrae Mariae*—Mary's Land—named for King Charles's French wife, Henrietta Maria. They sailed in two ships, the *Ark* and the *Dove*, and established Maryland's first capital at St. Mary's.

Historically, this was a major tobacco-growing region. Far less of the crop is grown today, though you still see occasional fields and tobacco barns around the countryside. You may also come across horse-drawn buggies, as there are considerable Amish settlements in the region.

Because of its tobacco plantations, the Maryland Tidewater was sympathetic to the Confederacy, and thus John Wilkes Booth fled through Charles County after assassinating President Abraham Lincoln at Ford's Theatre on April 14, 1865. He fled on horse over Navy Yard Bridge and had Dr. Samuel Mudd set his broken leg near La Plata. Booth and co-conspirator David Herold hid in a pine thicket for five days between Chapel Point and Zekiah Swamp, waiting for their chance to cross the Potomac on April 21. They were caught at the Garrett Farm, south of Port Royal, Virginia, where Booth was shot and killed on April 26.

Charles County has more wetlands than any other county in the Washington metropolitan area. Zekiah Swamp is Maryland's largest freshwater swamp (a swamp is a flooded woodland). It empties into the Wicomico River, a tidal tributary to the Potomac. This beautiful primeval forest is accessible via canoe.

St. Mary's County has a large number of historic churches, many from the seventeenth and eighteenth centuries, reflecting the county's diverse and sometimes divisive conflict between Anglicans and Catholics, as well as segregation against African Americans.

# Chapel Point State Park

Chapel Point overlooks the confluence of the Potomac and Port Tobacco Rivers. Father Andrew White, the Jesuit priest who accompanied the first Catholic settlers, picked this site with its splendid view for a chapel in 1641. It was close to a Piscataway Indian village Potopaco, now known as Port Tobacco. St. Ignatius is the oldest continuously operating parish in the United States.

Three buildings form the parish: the sacristy (1662), the Georgian manor (1741) and the modest brick church (1789). A fire destroyed much of the interior in 1866, but the church was reconstructed. There is a lovely cemetery stretching downhill toward the rivers. A two-sided memorial commemorates the English Jesuits who served in North America. St. Ignatius is home to a relic, supposedly a sliver of the true cross, which makes this church a pilgrim destination. Andrew White carried the relic as he ministered to the English settlers and Piscataway Indians.

## *Port Tobacco*

A few miles north of Chapel Point are the remnants of Port Tobacco, established about 1727. Like many places in the Tidewater region, tobacco farming silted in the Port Tobacco River, preventing ships from reaching the port. Still, it remained the seat of Charles County government until 1896. Reconstructed buildings include the Port Tobacco Courthouse.

## *Thomas Stone National Historic Site*

Although not on the Potomac, the Thomas Stone National Historic Site (6655 Rose Hill Road) is a few miles north of Port Tobacco and worth a visit. Stone was one of the four Maryland delegates who signed the Declaration of Independence. His home, Haverventure, is in excellent condition; there is a family cemetery and 1.5 miles of trails through the wooded property.

*How to get there: St. Ignatius Church is thirty-five miles south of Washington. Follow Route 5 south to U.S. 301 south to La Plata. Four miles south of La Plata, turn right onto Chapel Point Road.*

# ST. CLEMENT'S ISLAND STATE PARK

On March 25, 1634, about 140 Catholic settlers led by Leonard Calvert, younger brother of Cecil Calvert, Lord Baltimore, landed on this wooded island. Father Andrew White celebrated the first Catholic mass spoken in English in North America. Calvert soon met with the Piscataway Indians, the dominant tribe in the region, who were peaceful but less than enthusiastic about the newcomers. He decided to settle farther down the river at St. Mary's, and the settlers decamped.

St. Clement's Island is a mile offshore from Coltons Point, home to the St. Clement's Island–Potomac River Museum. The island eroded significantly and is down to forty acres from its original four hundred, and for much of its history

The first English Catholic settlers sailed into the Potomac in 1634 and landed on St. Clement's Island. *Garrett Peck.*

it was known as Blackistone Island. The Blackistone Lighthouse was built in 1851 to help ships navigate the river. It was decommissioned in 1932 and burned down in 1956. The lighthouse was rebuilt in 2008.

A water taxi operates between the museum at Coltons Point and the island from May to October. The island has 2.5 miles of walking paths that take you to the site of the Blackistone Canning Company, several ponds, an osprey rookery, a forty-foot cross commemorating the 1634 landing and the rebuilt lighthouse.

*How to get there: St. Clement's Island State Park is at 38370 Point Breeze Road in Coltons Point, Maryland.*

# Piney Point Lighthouse

Out of five surviving lighthouses on the Potomac, Piney Point Lighthouse is the most endearing. A two-story, stubby brick fixture built in 1836, the lighthouse is open to the public. A steep staircase takes you to the top. The keeper's quarters are next door, and nearby is the Potomac River Maritime Exhibit Building. During World War II, torpedoes from the Torpedo Factory in Alexandria were tested at Piney Point. After the war, a captured German submarine, the *U-1105*, was sunk a mile offshore in 1949 in a navy demolition test. It is a popular site for divers. Piney Point is also a fishing point for ospreys from March to October (the birds migrate to South America during the winter).

Continuing south along Highway 249 from Piney Point leads you to St. George Island. In July 1776, the last royal governor of Virginia, John Murray, Earl of Dunmore, gathered a fleet of seventy-two ships at the island to gather supplies and water. Many of his ships were ill-equipped, some manned by slaves to whom he had promised freedom. The St. Mary's militia made life difficult for the British, and after smallpox broke out, Dunmore scuttled twenty of the ships and sailed away on August 2.

A couple miles northeast of Piney Point is the Drayden African American Schoolhouse (18287 Cherryfield Road in Drayden). It is an intact one-room schoolhouse built in 1890 and used until 1944, an era when St. Mary's County schools were segregated.

*How to get there: Piney Point Lighthouse is at 44720 Lighthouse Road in Piney Point, Maryland.*

# HISTORIC ST. MARY'S CITY

In 1634, two ships, the *Ark* and the *Dove*, sailed up the Potomac with 140 English Catholic settlers led by Leonard Calvert. They met with the local Piscataway Indians and decided to settle near the Potomac's mouth. This settlement was up a two-mile inlet, the St. Mary's River. The town of St. Mary's became Maryland's capital, as well as the first colony to mandate religious toleration. The capital moved to Annapolis in 1694.

Historic St. Mary's City is a reproduction of the colonial capital, like Jamestown and Williamsburg in Virginia. It encompasses eight hundred acres. There is a reconstructed 1676 statehouse, a tobacco plantation, a replica of the *Dove* and an Indian village. The rebuilt Brick Chapel of 1667 is a Baroque Catholic chapel that the Maryland governor ordered demolished in 1704; the Jesuits used the bricks to build a manor house in St. Inigoes nearby in 1785. Living historians reenact characters from the seventeenth century.

Adjacent to the historic district is St. Mary's College—the real reason the town exists today. Trinity Episcopal Church was first built in 1638 for Anglican settlers near St. Mary's; the current church was constructed in 1829 using bricks from the demolished statehouse. St. John's Site Archaeology Museum demonstrates the archaeological finds from the colonial town.

*How to get there: Historic St. Mary's City is seventy miles from Washington, D.C., along Maryland Route 5.*

# POINT LOOKOUT STATE PARK

Point Lookout is a thin peninsula that marks the Potomac's end as it flows into the Chesapeake Bay. A lighthouse was built there in 1830 and operated until 1966, often tended by female lighthouse keepers. Hammond General Hospital, large enough to support 1,400 patients, was opened in 1862 during the Civil War. After the Battle of Gettysburg the following year, the Union constructed Camp Hoffman, the largest prisoner of war camp during the war, half a mile north of the point. About fifty-two thousand Confederates were imprisoned in the stockade, guarded by the still extant Fort Lincoln. Both the camp and hospital were closed at the end of the war.

Point Lookout was so isolated that the Confederates were practically immune from escape or rescue. They were not immune to the harsh winter

A Civil War–era image of Point Lookout. The star-shaped building is Hammond General Hospital. *Library of Congress.*

weather: most of the prisoners slept on the ground, having neither tents nor barracks. Many were improperly clothed. High tide often flooded the camp, and sanitation was nonexistent. By the end of the Civil War, four thousand men had died of disease and starvation. They were buried in a mass grave.

Most of the POW camp has eroded into Chesapeake Bay, and the Point Lookout Confederate Cemetery has been moved twice. There are two obelisks over the cemetery listing the names of the dead. The state park offers a Civil War Museum/Marshland Nature Center, as well as a small beach. Point Lookout is popular for bird watching, boating, camping, cycling and fishing.

*How to get there: Point Lookout is eighty miles from Washington, D.C. Take Maryland Route 5 south until it dead-ends at the park.*

# Additional Reading

Achenbach, Joel. *The Grand Idea: George Washington's Potomac and the Race to the West*. New York: Simon & Schuster, 2004.

Berg, Scott. *Grand Avenues: The Story of the French Visionary Who Designed Washington, D.C.* New York: Pantheon, 2007.

Bordewich, Fergus M. *Washington: The Making of the American Capital*. New York: Amistad, 2008.

Bornemann, Walter. *1812: The War that Forged a Nation*. New York: HarperCollins, 2004.

Brezinski, David K. *Geology of the Sideling Hill Road Cut*. Baltimore: Maryland Geological Survey, 1994.

Brown, Gordon S. *The Captain Who Burned His Ships: Captain Thomas Tingey, USN, 1750–1829*. Annapolis, MD: Naval Institute Press, 2011.

Chernow, Ron. *Washington: A Life*. New York: Penguin, 2010.

Douglas, Henry Kyd. *I Rode with Stonewall*. Chapel Hill: University of North Carolina Press, 1940.

Gilmore, Matthew, and Joshua Olsen. *Foggy Bottom and the West End*. Charleston, SC: The History Press, 2010.

Hanel, Selma I. *Carderock, Past and Present: A Climber's Guide*. Vienna, VA: Potomac Appalachian Trail Club, 1990.

High, Mike. *The C&O Canal Companion*. Updated edition. Baltimore, MD: Johns Hopkins University Press, 2000.

Horwitz, Tony. *Midnight Rising: John Brown and the Raid that Sparked the Civil War*. New York: Henry Holt, 2011.

Hutchinson, Louise Daniel. *The Anacostia Story: 1608–1930*. Washington, D.C.: Smithsonian Institution Press, 1977.

Kennedy, Frances, ed. *The Civil War Battlefield Guide*. 2nd ed. New York: Houghton Mifflin Company, 1998.

McPherson, James M. *Battle Cry of Freedom: The Civil War Era*. New York: Ballantine Books, 1988.

———. *Crossroads of Freedom*. New York: Oxford University Press, 2002.

Metcalf, Paul. *Waters of Potowmack*. Charlottesville: University of Virginia Press, 2002.

Morgan, James A., III. *A Little Short of Boats: The Battles of Ball's Bluff and Edwards Ferry, October 21–22, 1861*. El Dorado Hills, CA: Savas Beatie, 2011.

National Park Service. *Underground Railroad*. National Park Service handbook, 1998.

Pogue, Dennis J. *Founding Spirits: George Washington and the Beginnings of the American Whiskey Industry*. Buena Vista, VA: Harbour Books, 2011.

Pope, Michael Lee. *Hidden History of Alexandria, D.C.* Charleston, SC: The History Press, 2011.

Prud'homme, Alex. *The Ripple Effect: The Fate of Freshwater in the Twenty-first Century*. New York: Scribner, 2011.

Ramage, James A. *Gray Ghost: The Life of Col. John Singleton Mosby*. Lexington: University Press of Kentucky, 1999.

Savage, Kirk. *Monument Wars: Washington, D.C., the National Mall, and the Transformation of the Memorial Landscape*. Berkeley and Los Angeles: University of California Press, 2009.

Sears, Stephen W. *Landscape Turned Red: The Battle of Antietam*. New York: Ticknor & Fields, 1983.

Stanton, Richard L. *Potomac Journey: Fairfax Stone to Tidewater*. Washington, D.C.: Smithsonian Institution Press, 1993.

Swanson, James L. *Manhunt: The Twelve-Day Chase for Lincoln's Killer*. New York: HarperCollins, 2006.

Tanner, Robert G. *Stonewall in the Valley: Thomas J. "Stonewall" Jackson's Shenandoah Valley Campaign, Spring 1862*. Mechanicsburg, PA: Stackpole Books, 1996.

Tilp, Frederick. *This Was Potomac River*. Alexandria, VA: Tilp, 1978.

Wennersten, John R. *Anacostia: The Death and Life of an American River*. Baltimore, MD: Chesapeake Book Company, 2008.

Wills, Mary Alice. *The Confederate Blockade of Washington, D.C. 1861–1862*. Parsons, WV: McClain Printing Company, 1975.

# Index

Index

# About the Author

G arrett Peck falls down Georgetown's *Exorcist* stairs every chance he gets, yet he can't exorcise his passion for history. A literary journalist and history dork, he is the author of *The Prohibition Hangover: Alcohol in America from Demon Rum to Cult Cabernet* and *Prohibition in Washington, D.C.: How Dry We Weren't* and leads the Temperance Tour of prohibition-related sites in Washington. *The Potomac River: A History and Guide* is his third book. A native Californian and a Virginia Military Institute graduate, he lives in lovely Arlington, Virginia. www.garrettpeck.com.